Holt Adapted Reader

Instruction in Reading Literature and Informational Texts

HOLT, RINEHART AND WINSTON

A Harcourt Education Company

Orlando • **Austin** • New York • San Diego • Toronto • London

7 8 9 10 11 179 09 08 07 06

Contents

Skills Table of Contents

Reading Skills

Literary Skills

Vocabulary Skills

To the Student

A Book for You

Imagine this: a book full of great stories and interesting texts. Make it a book that actually tells you to write in it. Fill it with graphic organizers that encourage you to think a different way. Make it a size that's easy to carry around. That's *Holt Adapted Reader*—a book created especially for you.

In *Holt Adapted Reader* you will find two kinds of selections—original literature and adaptations. Original literature is exactly what appears in *Elements of Literature*, Third Course. All the poems and plays in this book are examples of original literature. As you read original literature, you will find two kinds of helps — **YOU NEED TO KNOW** and **IN OTHER WORDS**. You Need to Know gives you background information about the work. It also explains some of the work's main ideas. In Other Words paraphrases the text that comes before it. That is, it restates the text in different words.

Adaptations are based on stories or articles that appear in *Elements of Literature,* Third Course. Adaptations make the selections more accessible to all readers. You can easily identify any selection that is an adaptation. Just look for the words *based on* in the Table of Contents.

Learning to Read Literary and Informational Texts

When you read informational texts like a social studies textbook or a newspaper article, you usually read to get the facts. You read mainly to get information that is stated directly on the page. When you read literature, you need to go beyond the words on the page. You need to read between the lines of a poem or story to discover the writer's meaning. No matter what kind of reading you do, *Holt Adapted Reader* will help you practice the skills and strategies you need to become an active and successful reader.

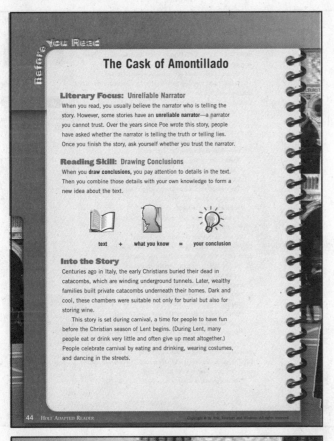

Before You Read

On the Before You Read page you will preview the two skills you will practice as you read the selection.

- In the **Literary Focus** you will learn about one literary element—such as character or rhyme. This literary element is one you will see in the selection.
- The **Reading Skill** presents a key skill that you will learn and practice as you read the selection.

The Before You Read page also introduces you to the reading selection.

- **Into the Story** (or another genre) gives you background information. This information will help you understand the selection or its author. It may also help you understand the time period in which the story was written.

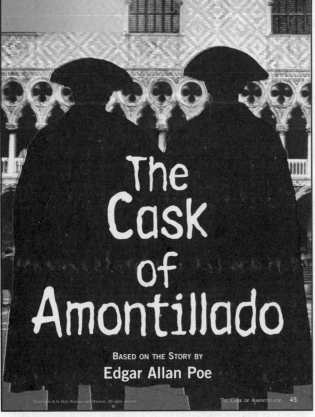

Interactive Selections from
Elements of Literature

The readings are some of the same ones that appear in *Elements of Literature*, Third Course. Some are adaptations of selections in *Elements of Literature*. The selections are printed to give you the room you need to mark up the text.

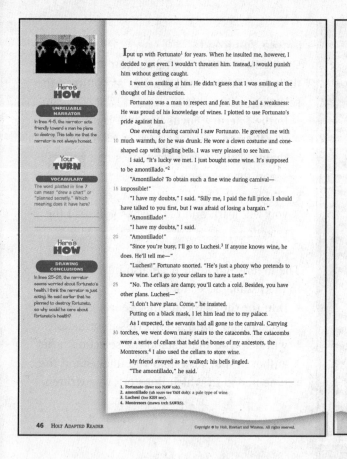

Here's HOW

UNRELIABLE NARRATOR

In lines 4–5, the narrator acts friendly toward a man he plans to destroy. This tells me that the narrator is not always honest.

Your TURN

VOCABULARY

The word *plotted* in line 7 can mean "drew a chart" or "planned secretly." Which meaning does it have here?

Here's HOW

DRAWING CONCLUSIONS

In lines 25–28, the narrator seems worried about Fortunato's health. I think the narrator is just acting. He said earlier that he planned to destroy Fortunato, so why would he care about Fortunato's health?

I put up with Fortunato[1] for years. When he insulted me, however, I decided to get even. I wouldn't threaten him. Instead, I would punish him without getting caught.

I went on smiling at him. He didn't guess that I was smiling at the
5 thought of his destruction.

Fortunato was a man to respect and fear. But he had a weakness: He was proud of his knowledge of wines. I plotted to use Fortunato's pride against him.

One evening during carnival I saw Fortunato. He greeted me with
10 much warmth, for he was drunk. He wore a clown costume and cone-shaped cap with jingling bells. I was very pleased to see him.

I said, "It's lucky we met. I just bought some wine. It's supposed to be amontillado."[2]

"Amontillado? To obtain such a fine wine during carnival—
15 impossible!"

"I have my doubts," I said. "Silly me, I paid the full price. I should have talked to you first, but I was afraid of losing a bargain."

"Amontillado!"

"I have my doubts," I said.
20 "Amontillado!"

"Since you're busy, I'll go to Luchesi.[3] If anyone knows wine, he does. He'll tell me—"

"Luchesi!" Fortunato snorted. "He's just a phony who pretends to know wine. Let's go to your cellars to have a taste."

25 "No. The cellars are damp; you'll catch a cold. Besides, you have other plans. Luchesi—"

"I don't have plans. Come," he insisted.

Putting on a black mask, I let him lead me to my palace.

As I expected, the servants had all gone to the carnival. Carrying
30 torches, we went down many stairs to the catacombs. The catacombs were a series of cellars that held the bones of my ancestors, the Montresors.[4] I also used the cellars to store wine.

My friend swayed as he walked; his bells jingled.

"The amontillado," he said.

---

1. **Fortunato** (fawr too NAW toh).
2. **amontillado** (uh mawn tee YAH doh): a pale type of wine.
3. **Luchesi** (loo KEH see).
4. **Montresors** (mawn treh SAWRS).

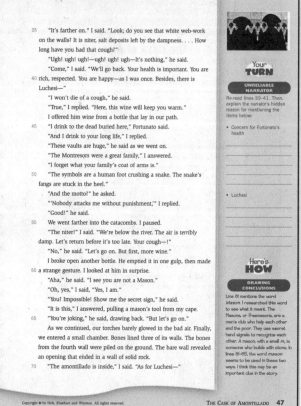

35 "It's farther on." I said. "Look; do you see that white web-work on the walls? It is niter, salt deposits left by the dampness. . . . How long have you had that cough?"

"Ugh! ugh! ugh!—ugh! ugh! ugh—It's nothing," he said.

"Come," I said. "We'll go back. Your health is important. You are
40 rich, respected. You are happy—as I was once. Besides, there is Luchesi—"

"I won't die of a cough," he said.

"True," I replied. "Here, this wine will keep you warm." I offered him wine from a bottle that lay in our path.

45 "I drink to the dead buried here," Fortunato said.

"And I drink to your long life," I replied.

"These vaults are huge," he said as we went on.

"The Montresors were a great family," I answered.

"I forget what your family's coat of arms is."

50 "The symbols are a human foot crushing a snake. The snake's fangs are stuck in the heel."

"And the motto?" he asked.

"'Nobody attacks me without punishment,'" I replied.

"Good!" he said.

55 We went farther into the catacombs. I paused.

"The niter!" I said. "We're below the river. The air is *terribly* damp. Let's return before it's too late. Your cough—!"

"No," he said. "Let's go on. But first, more wine."

I broke open another bottle. He emptied it in one gulp, then made
60 a strange gesture. I looked at him in surprise.

"Aha," he said. "I see you are not a Mason."

"Oh, yes," I said, "Yes, I am."

"You? Impossible! Show me the secret sign," he said.

"It is this," I answered, pulling a mason's tool from my cape.

65 "You're joking," he said, drawing back. "But let's go on."

As we continued, our torches barely glowed in the bad air. Finally, we entered a small chamber. Bones lined three of its walls. The bones from the fourth wall were piled on the ground. The bare wall revealed an opening that ended in a wall of solid rock.

70 "The amontillado is inside," I said. "As for Luchesi—"

Here's HOW

DRAWING CONCLUSIONS

Line 61 mentions the word *Mason*. I researched this word to see what it meant. The Masons, or Freemasons, are a men's club who help each other and the poor. They use secret hand signals to recognize each other. A mason, with a small m, is someone who builds with stone. In lines 61–65, the word *mason* seems to be used in these two ways. I think this may be an important clue in the story.

THE CASK OF AMONTILLADO **47**

Strategies to Guide Your Reading: Side Notes

The **Here's HOW** feature models, or shows you, how to apply a particular skill to what you are reading. This feature lets you see how another person might think about the text. Each Here's HOW focuses on a reading skill, a literary skill, or a vocabulary skill.

The **Your TURN** feature gives you a chance to practice a skill on your own. Each Your TURN focuses on a reading skill, a literary skill, or a vocabulary skill. You might be asked to underline or circle words in the text. You might also be asked to write your response to a question on lines that are provided for you.

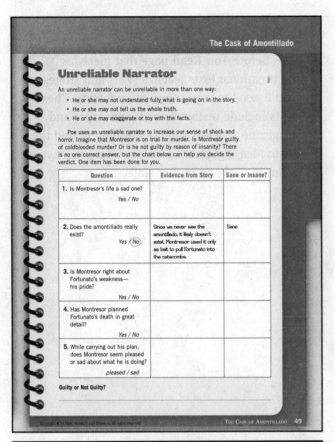

Graphic Organizers

After each selection is a **graphic organizer.** These organizers give you another way to understand the reading skill or literary focus of the selection. You might be asked to chart the main events of the plot or complete a cause-and-effect chain.

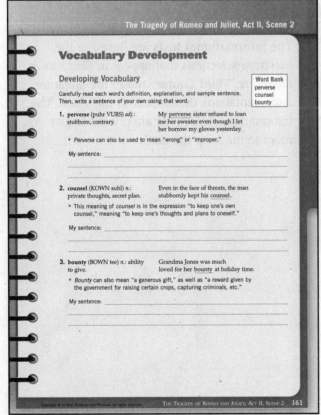

Vocabulary Development

Vocabulary Development worksheets appear at the end of some literary selections. These worksheets help you develop skills for building vocabulary.

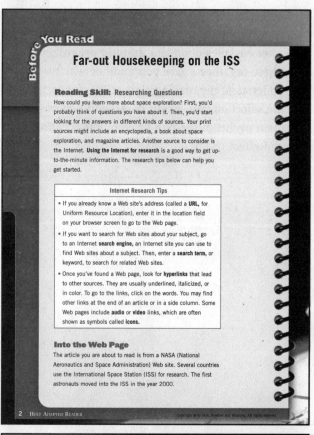

Before You Read

The **Before You Read** page that precedes informational texts teaches skills and strategies you'll need to read informational texts. These texts include textbooks and newspaper and magazine articles. You'll learn how to find the main idea, figure out an author's perspective or point of view, and other skills.

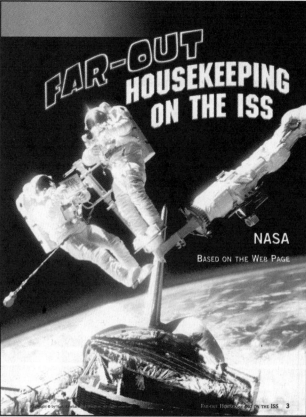

Interactive Informational Texts

The **informational texts** are linked to the literature selections that appear in *Elements of Literature,* Third Course, and to the literature and adaptations that appear in this book. The informational selections are printed to give you room to mark up the text.

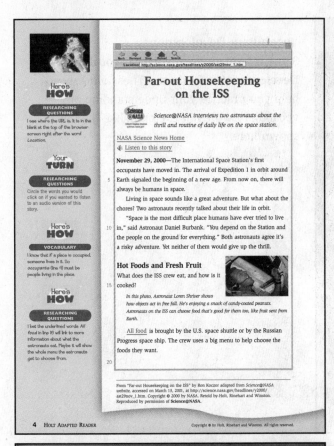

Side Notes

Notes in the side column accompany each selection. They guide your experience with the text and help you unlock meaning. Many notes ask you to circle or underline in the text itself.

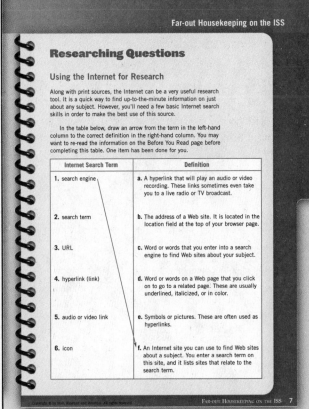

Graphic Organizers

After each selection, a **graphic organizer** gives you another way to understand the selection. These organizers focus on the skill introduced on the Before You Read page. You might be asked to collect supporting details that point to a main idea or to complete a comparison chart.

A Walk Through   Reading Informational Texts

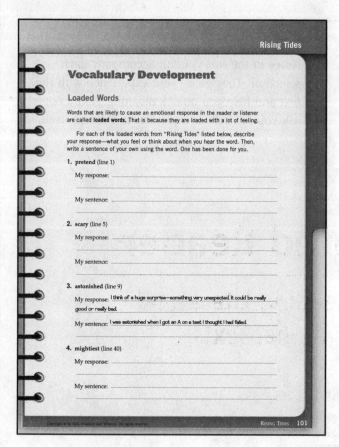

Vocabulary Development

Some informational texts have **Vocabulary Development** worksheets. These worksheets help you practice your understanding of vocabulary words in exercises like the one shown here.

Holt Adapted Reader

Instruction in Reading Literature and Informational Texts

Far-out Housekeeping on the ISS

Reading Skill: Researching Questions

How could you learn more about space exploration? First, you'd probably think of questions you have about it. Then, you'd start looking for the answers in different kinds of sources. Your print sources might include an encyclopedia, a book about space exploration, and magazine articles. Another source to consider is the Internet. **Using the Internet for research** is a good way to get up-to-the-minute information. The research tips below can help you get started.

Internet Research Tips

- If you already know a Web site's address (called a **URL,** for Uniform Resource Location), enter it in the location field on your browser screen to go to the Web page.

- If you want to search for Web sites about your subject, go to an Internet **search engine,** an Internet site you can use to find Web sites about a subject. Then, enter a **search term,** or keyword, to search for related Web sites.

- Once you've found a Web page, look for **hyperlinks** that lead to other sources. They are usually underlined, italicized, or in color. To go to the links, click on the words. You may find other links at the end of an article or in a side column. Some Web pages include **audio** or **video** links, which are often shown as symbols called **icons.**

Into the Web Page

The article you are about to read is from a NASA (National Aeronautics and Space Administration) Web site. Several countries use the International Space Station (ISS) for research. The first astronauts moved into the ISS in the year 2000.

FAR-OUT HOUSEKEEPING ON THE ISS

NASA

BASED ON THE WEB PAGE

Your
TURN

RESEARCHING QUESTIONS

Circle the words you would click on if you wanted to listen to an audio version of this story.

Here's
HOW

VOCABULARY

I know that if a place is occupied, someone lives in it. So *occupants* (line 4) must be people living in the place.

Here's
HOW

RESEARCHING QUESTIONS

I bet the underlined words *All food* in line 16 will link to more information about what the astronauts eat. Maybe it will show the whole menu the astronauts get to choose from.

Location: http://science.nasa.gov/headlines/y2000/ast29nov_1.htm

Far-out Housekeeping on the ISS

Science@NASA interviews two astronauts about the thrill and routine of daily life on the space station.

NASA Science News Home

◁€ Listen to this story

November 29, 2000—The International Space Station's first occupants have moved in. The arrival of Expedition 1 in orbit around
5   Earth signaled the beginning of a new age. From now on, there will always be humans in space.

Living in space sounds like a great adventure. But what about the chores? Two astronauts recently talked about their life in orbit.

"Space is the most difficult place humans have ever tried to live
10 in," said Astronaut Daniel Burbank. "You depend on the Station and the people on the ground for everything." Both astronauts agree it's a risky adventure. Yet neither of them would give up the thrill.

Hot Foods and Fresh Fruit

What does the ISS crew eat, and how is it
15 cooked?

In this photo, Astronaut Loren Shriver shows how objects act in free fall. He's enjoying a snack of candy-coated peanuts. Astronauts on the ISS can choose food that's good for them too, like fruit sent from Earth.

<u>All food</u> is brought by the U.S. space shuttle or by the Russian Progress space ship. The crew uses a big menu to help choose the foods they want.

According to Vicki Kloeris, the food manager, most food on the
20 ISS will come packaged in bags or cans. The astronauts will have to

---

From "Far-out Housekeeping on the ISS" by Ron Koczor adapted from *Science@NASA website*, accessed on March 13, 2001, at http://science.nasa.gov/headlines/y2000/ast29nov_1.htm. Copyright © 2000 by NASA. Retold by Holt, Rinehart and Winston. Reproduced by permission of **Science@NASA**.

add hot water to dried food. They will simply heat and eat other food. There will be a small amount of fresh fruit and vegetables. Nothing will need to be kept cold. Food is cooked on a small food warmer that is about the size of a suitcase.

ISS, Phone Home

25

Crews on the Russian Mir[1] space station found that feeling alone and being separated from people they cared about was one of their biggest problems. To prevent this on ISS, crew members will be encouraged to phone home. Each crew

30 member will have a video telephone call from home every week. The crew will also receive and send daily e-mail from family and friends.

Members of the STS-106 crew[2] took this photo of the ISS from the space shuttle Atlantis *in September 2000.* [<u>more information</u>]

Who Takes Out the Trash?

A story about <u>water recycling on the ISS</u> recently appeared on

35 Science@NASA. It covered the ways ISS designers are trying to lessen the number of things that must be brought from Earth. The goal is to recycle, that is, return for further use, 95% of the water used on the ISS. But other things can't be recycled as well as water can. So: Who takes out the trash?

40 The Russian Progress and the U.S. shuttle come to the rescue. The shuttle arrives with fresh supplies. On its return trip to Earth, it takes bags and containers of sealed trash. The Russian Progress gets rid of trash in a more exciting way. After the trash bags are piled in, the Progress is sealed. It is placed in a lower orbit and it and the

45 trash are burned up over the ocean.

---

1. **Mir** (MEER): a Russian space station no longer in use.
2. **STS-106 crew:** a number that identifies the mission. Each shuttle is used for many missions.

Your TURN

RESEARCHING QUESTIONS

What would you expect to learn by clicking on the words *more information* in the photo caption?

_____

_____

_____

_____

_____

_____

_____

Here's HOW

RESEARCHING QUESTIONS

These links are pretty handy. If I wanted to read that story about how they recycle water on the space station, I'd click on the underlined words in line 34.

Here's HOW

RESEARCHING QUESTIONS

There are no links to all the explorers who came before the astronauts (lines 53-57). I remember reading about some of them in my social studies class. I'm sure I could find more information in the encyclopedia in the library. I could also enter a keyword like *explorers* into an Internet search engine.

Your TURN

RESEARCHING QUESTIONS

Look at the Web links listed in lines 64–75. If you wanted more general information on the ISS, which link would you click on? Put a check mark next to the link you would use.

Back Forward Stop Reload Search

Location: http://science.nasa.gov/headlines/y2000/ast29nov_1.htm

R & R in Space

Crews will be busy on the ISS. But how will the men and women on the space ship rest and relax?

50 "Crew members will be allowed to take a certain amount of personal gear up with them," said Astronaut Edward Lu. They can have things like checkers, chess, CDs, tape players, and DVD movies.

It's not exactly like home, and you can't take a walk outside. But the "sailors" on ISS will have it better than the brave explorers who came before them, such as the Europeans in the 15th century who 55 looked for new lands, Polynesian sailors who mapped and settled the islands of the Pacific Ocean, and Asian explorers and settlers who walked the land bridge from Siberia into Alaska.

The astronauts and those earlier explorers share two important qualities. First, they are the vanguard, the pioneers. They are doing 60 what they believe will improve the lives of their people.

Second, they all had to move ahead and ignore the voices behind them warning that "beyond this point, there are dragons!"[3]

Web Links

Water on the Space Station —The first Science@NASA article in this 65 series. It's about the problems that come from living in space for a long time. This article looks at how water is saved and reused on the space station. Even the water in the crew's urine is saved and reused.
Breathing Easy on the Space Station —The second Science@NASA article in this series. It's also about the problems that come from 70 living in space for a long time. This article looks at the methods used to make sure the crew gets safe, breathable air.
Microscopic Stowaways on the Space Station —The third Science@ NASA article in this series about living in space for a long time.
International Space Station —NASA's Web page for the International 75 Space Station.

---

3. "... are dragons!": meaning "unexplored territory." Similar words are found on maps of early European explorations in the areas beyond known lands.

Researching Questions

Using the Internet for Research

Along with print sources, the Internet can be a very useful research tool. It is a quick way to find up-to-the-minute information on just about any subject. However, you'll need a few basic Internet search skills in order to make the best use of this source.

In the table below, draw an arrow from the term in the left-hand column to the correct definition in the right-hand column. You may want to re-read the information on the Before You Read page before completing this table. One item has been done for you.

Internet Search Term	Definition
1. search engine	a. A hyperlink that will play an audio or video recording. These links sometimes even take you to a live radio or TV broadcast.
2. search term	b. The address of a Web site. It is located in the location field at the top of your browser page.
3. URL	c. Word or words that you enter into a search engine to find Web sites about your subject.
4. hyperlink (link)	d. Word or words on a Web page that you click on to go to a related page. These are usually underlined, italicized, or in color.
5. audio or video link	e. Symbols or pictures. These are often used as hyperlinks.
6. icon	f. An Internet site you can use to find Web sites about a subject. You enter a search term on this site, and it lists sites that relate to the search term.

A Christmas Memory

Literary Focus: Setting

Setting makes a story real. **Setting** is the time and place of a story. It can include the weather and the customs of the people—how they live, what they eat, how they dress, and what they believe. Setting can help reveal character, affect the plot, add to the **mood** (or feeling), and contribute to the meaning of the story. Truman Capote's descriptions of the setting are a vital part of his story.

Reading Skill: Reading for Details

You can learn a lot from the details of a story, especially from the **sensory details**—images that appeal to your senses of sight, hearing, touch, taste, and smell. These details help make the story come alive. They also help establish the feeling, or **mood,** of the story.

Sensory Details

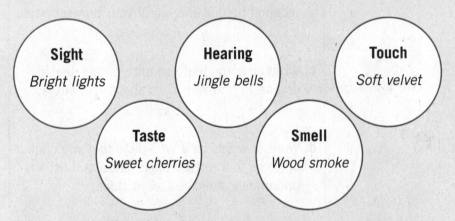

Sight Bright lights	**Hearing** Jingle bells	**Touch** Soft velvet
	Taste Sweet cherries	**Smell** Wood smoke

Into the Short Story

This story is partly autobiographical—some of the details really happened to the author. The story is set in the countryside in the South during the Depression of the early 1930s. It is about friendship and the enduring power of love—even when, to the rest of the world, the friendship seems odd, and the love is not even noticed at all.

A Christmas Memory

BASED ON THE STORY BY
Truman Capote

Imagine a morning in late November—a morning more than twenty years ago. Imagine the kitchen in an old country house. In the room is a large black stove. There is also a round table and a fireplace. Two rocking chairs stand by the fireplace. Today's fire is the first of the
5 season.

A small, white-haired woman stands at the window. She wears tennis shoes, and a baggy gray sweater covers a summer dress. Her shoulders hunch from a long childhood illness. Like Lincoln's, her face is craggy and tanned by sun and wind. It's delicate, too. Her eyes
10 are golden brown and timid. "Oh my," she says, "It's fruitcake weather!"

I'm seven, and she is sixty-something. We are distant cousins and live together with other relatives who have power over us. She and I are best friends. She calls me Buddy after a childhood friend who died
15 in the 1880s when she was a child. She is still a child.

"We have thirty cakes to bake," she said.

We push a worn-out baby carriage to the pecan trees. The wheels wobble like a drunk's legs, but we use it to carry a lot of things. Queenie, our little orange and white rat terrier, sleeps in it.

20 Later we shell a huge buggyload of pecans. Our backs hurt from picking up pecans, and we sigh when we toss the last shell into the fire and watch it catch flame. The buggy is empty, but the bowl is full.

We eat supper and discuss tomorrow. Tomorrow we'll buy
25 cherries, citron, ginger, vanilla, and pineapple. We'll buy rinds, raisins, walnuts, and whiskey. We'll buy flour, butter, eggs, and spices. We'll need a pony to pull the buggy!

But first there is the question of money. We've earned some from selling things. We sell junk, blackberries, jam, and flowers. Once we
30 won five dollars in a football contest. We're hoping for a fifty-thousand-dollar Grand Prize for naming a new coffee. (We suggested "A.M." and the slogan "A.M.! Amen!") We did best with the Fun and Freak Museum. The Fun was a slide show of Washington and New York, and the Freak was a young three-legged chicken. Everybody

"A Christmas Memory" story adapted from *Breakfast at Tiffanys* by Truman Capote. Copyright ©1956 by Truman Capote. Retold by Holt, Rinehart and Winston. Reproduced by permission of **Random House, Inc.**

around wanted to see that chick. We charged adults a nickel, kids two cents. We made twenty dollars before the chick died.

But somehow we've always save up a Fruitcake Fund. The money is kept hidden under my friend's bed.

On my friend's quilt, we dump out the money. Dollar bills are
40 rolled as tightly as spring buds. There are fifty-cent pieces heavy enough to weight a dead man's eyes. There are lovely dimes—the coin that really jingles—and nickels and quarters worn smooth as creek pebbles. Finally, there is $13.00 in bitter-smelling pennies. (We earned them for killing flies.) My friend is upset because thirteen is
45 unlucky. She always spends thirteenths in bed. To be safe, we toss a penny out the window.

Whiskey is the most expensive cake ingredient. It's also the hardest to get because it's illegal. Everybody buys it from Mr. Haha Jones. The next day we finished our other shopping and set out for
50 Mr. Haha's. People say his cafe by the river is "sinful." They call him Haha because he is a gloomy giant who never laughs. We've never seen him because we've always dealt with his wife. His cafe's a large log cabin with chains of naked light bulbs hanging around it. It stands by the river's muddy edge. At night, people have been murdered in
55 Haha's—hit on the head, cut to pieces. During the day, it is shabby and empty. I knock at the door.

Footsteps. Mr. Haha Jones himself opens the door! And he *is* a giant, and he *doesn't* smile. He frowns at us through Satan-tilted eyes. "What you want with Haha?" he asks.

60 My friend finds her voice. "Please, Mr. Haha, we'd like a quart of your finest whiskey," she says.

Haha is smiling—laughing, too. "Which of you is a drinking man?"

"It's for making fruitcakes, Mr. Haha."

65 He frowns and says, "That's no way to waste good whiskey." Nonetheless, he brings us a bottle of daisy-yellow liquor. It sparkles in the sunlight. He says: "Two dollars."

We pay him with nickels, dimes, and pennies. Jiggling the coins like dice, he smiles and returns the money. "Send me a fruitcake
70 instead," he says.

Your TURN

READING FOR DETAILS

Many sensory details are used to describe the money in lines 39–43. Underline details that appeal to sight, smell, hearing, and touch. Near each detail you underline, add the name of the appropriate sense.

Your TURN

SETTING

Underline the details that describe the setting of Mr. Haha's cafe (lines 52–56). What is the mood of this setting? That is, how does it make the characters or you feel?

_____

_____

_____

_____

_____

_____

_____

_____

Your TURN

READING FOR DETAILS

Lines 73–77 have details that appeal to all five senses. Circle a detail for sight, smell, touch, taste, and hearing. Write the name of the sense next to the detail. (Sometimes one detail can appeal to more than one sense.)

Your TURN

READING FOR DETAILS

What do the details in lines 78–84 reveal about the character of the writer's friend?

_____

_____

Your TURN

READING FOR DETAILS

Most everyone would agree that it is not a good idea to give whiskey to a seven-year-old. Do you think the relatives' reaction was reasonable, or do you think they overreacted? There is no one correct answer, but be sure to use details from the text in your response. Which answer do you think the writer would give?

_____

_____

_____

_____

_____

"Well," my friend says on our way home, "there's a lovely man. We'll put extra raisins in *his* cake."

The black stove glows like a lighted pumpkin. Eggbeaters whirl; spoons spin in bowls of butter and sugar; vanilla sweetens the air; ginger spices it. Melting, nose-tingling odors fill the kitchen and drift outside on puffs of chimney smoke. In four days our work is done. Thirty-one cakes, damp with whiskey, sit on shelves.

They are for friends, but not always neighbor friends. Most are for people we've met once—or not at all. These are people who have pleased us—people like President Roosevelt or the Reverend and Mrs. J. C. Lucey, Baptist missionaries to Borneo. Or the knife sharpener who passes through twice a year. Or Abner Packer, who drives the six o'clock bus from Mobile. Because my friend is shy with everyone but strangers, these strangers are our best friends.

Now the kitchen is empty. The cakes are gone. We mailed the last one yesterday. Buying stamps emptied our purse and we are broke. That makes me unhappy, but my friend insists on celebrating. We still have two inches of Haha's whiskey left. Queenie has a spoonful in her bowl of coffee. We divide the rest between two jelly glasses. Because we are both new to drinking straight whiskey, we make faces and shudder at the taste. By and by, we begin to sing. We sing different songs at the same time. I dance. I mean to tap dance in the movies. I watch my dancing shadow having fun. Our voices rock the china, and we giggle as if being tickled. Queenie rolls on her back, her paws plowing the air. I feel warm and sparky like crumbling logs. I'm carefree as the wind in the chimney. My friend dances around the stove, her tennis shoes squeaking on the floor.

Two relatives find us. They are very angry. Their powerful eyes scold us, and their tongues burn us. Listen to what they have to say: "A child of seven! Whiskey on his breath! Are you out of your mind? Feeding a child of seven whiskey! Must be loony! Road to ruin! Remember Cousin Kate? Uncle Charlie? Uncle Charlie's brother-in-law? Shame! Scandal! Kneel. Pray. Beg the Lord!"

Queenie sneaks under the stove. My friend stares at her shoes, her chin quivering. She blows her nose and runs to her room. Long after the town and house are asleep, she cries.

"Don't cry," I say, sitting on her bed. "Tomorrow we have to cut a tree." Finally, she straightens up. Queenie licks her cheeks. "I know where to find real pretty trees, and holly, too, with berries big as your
110 eyes. It's way off in the woods—farther than we've ever been. Papa used to bring us trees from there. I can't wait for morning."

Morning. Frost shines in the grass. The sun makes the silvered winter woods shine. A wild turkey calls, and a hog grunts in the undergrowth. Our clothes catch on thorns, burs, and briers. The path
115 unwinds through lemony sun pools. My friend shivers with glee and inhales the pine-heavy air. "We're almost there. Can you smell it, Buddy?" she asks, as though we're nearing an ocean.

It is a kind of ocean made up of scented acres of holiday trees and prickly-leafed holly with shiny red berries. My friend says, "The tree
120 should be twice as tall as a boy so that a boy can't steal the star." The one we pick is twice as tall as me.

Passersby praise the treasure in our buggy and ask where it came from. But my friend is sly. She just murmurs, "Over there." At home by the fire, Queenie sleeps till tomorrow, snoring like a human.

125 In the attic we find decorations—coils of tinsel gone gold with age, one silver star, and a rope of old, candylike light bulbs. They're not enough. We want our tree to blaze like a stained-glass window and droop with heavy snows of ornaments. We do what we've always done. We sit for days with scissors and crayons and stacks of colored
130 paper making our own ornaments.

We make family gifts, too. We make gifts for each other in secret. I want to buy her a pearl-handled knife, a radio, a pound of chocolate-covered cherries. Instead, I'm building her a kite. She would like to give me a bicycle. Instead, she's probably building me a kite.
135 She gave me a kite last year and the year before. She can always make a kite fly—even without enough breeze to move clouds.

Early Christmas morning we talk. "I made you another kite," she says. Then I say I made her one, too, and we laugh.

First, breakfast is everything you can think of—flapjacks and fried
140 squirrel, grits and honey from the comb. The food puts the others in a good mood. My friend and I are so eager to open presents that we can't eat a bite.

Your TURN

SETTING

Sensory details make the setting come alive as the two friends search for their Christmas tree. Underline these details in lines 112–117. Then, describe the mood this setting creates. What kind of day do you think the two friends are having?

_____

_____

_____

_____

_____

Here's HOW

SETTING

I know that the setting can include the customs of the people, so what the family has for breakfast (lines 139–141) is interesting. I think they must hunt for or grow most of their own food because you can't usually buy squirrel meat in the supermarket. And maybe they have beehives if they eat their honey from the comb. I also know that grits are a kind of cereal people in the South especially like. They are sure having a big breakfast. Since it puts people in a good mood, it must be a special meal for Christmas.

Your
TURN

`SETTING`

The two friends have a good time flying their kites. Write on the lines below the mood, or feeling, of this scene (lines 153–156). Then, circle details of the setting that contribute to that mood.

_____

_____

_____

Your
TURN

`READING FOR DETAILS`

Re-read lines 166–177. Describe on the lines below the mood of this ending to the story. Support your description with details from the story.

_____

_____

_____

_____

_____

_____

_____

_____

We open presents. I'm disappointed. Who wouldn't be? With socks, a Sunday school shirt, some handkerchiefs, a hand-me-down
145 sweater, and a subscription to a Sunday school magazine.

My friend does better. I think her best present is a sack of oranges. She, however, is proudest of a white wool shawl that her married sister knit. She *says* her best present is the kite I built—and it *is* very beautiful. The blue one she made me is even more beautiful.
150 Gold and green Good Conduct stars cover it and my name is painted on it.

"Buddy, the wind is blowing," my friend says.

We run to a pasture where Queenie buries her bones. (A year later Queenie will be buried there, too.) Through the waist-high grass, we
155 fly our kites. Content, sun-warmed, we lie in the grass. We peel oranges and watch the kites in the sky. I forget the socks and hand-me-down sweater. I'm as happy as if we'd won the coffee-naming contest.

My friend begins to talk. "I used to believe I'd have to die to see
160 God. It'd be like looking at a stained-glass window with the sun pouring through. You wouldn't notice it getting dark. Now I think people have seen Him all along in things just as they are." Her hand makes a circle, gathering clouds, the kites, the grass, and Queenie pawing dirt over her bone. "I could leave the world with today in my
165 eyes."

This is our last Christmas together.

Life separates us. Those Who Know Best send me to military school. I go through miserable bugle-blowing prisons and grim military-style summer camps. I have a new home too, but it doesn't
170 count. Home is where my friend is, and I never go there.

And she stays there puttering around the kitchen—alone with Queenie. Then alone. For a few Novembers, she bakes fruitcakes alone. She sends me "the best of the batch." One coming-of-winter morning, she no longer has the energy to say, "It's fruitcake weather!"
175 And when that happens, I know it. I'm like a kite on a broken string. On that December morning, I search the sky. I look for a lost pair of kites hurrying toward heaven.

Reading for Details

Truman Capote's "A Christmas Memory" is full of **sensory details**—images that appeal to the five senses. In the left-hand column of the chart below are descriptions of setting from the short story. In the right-hand column, state what senses—sight, smell, taste, touch, hearing—the details appeal to, and then state the **mood**—or feeling—of the setting. One has been done for you.

Description of Setting	Senses Appealed to and Mood
1. "In the room is a large black stove. There is also a round table and a fireplace. Two rocking chairs stand by the fireplace. Today's fire is the first of the season."	Senses: Mood:
2. "The black stove glows like a lighted pumpkin. Eggbeaters whirl; spoons spin in bowls of butter and sugar; vanilla sweetens the air; ginger spices it."	Senses: Mood:
3. "Morning. Frost shines in the grass. The sun makes the silvered winter woods shine. A wild turkey calls, and a hog grunts in the undergrowth. Our clothes catch on thorns, burs, and briers. The path unwinds through lemony sun pools."	Senses: Mood:
4. "Through the waist-high grass, we fly our kites. Content, sun-warmed, we lie in the grass. We peel oranges and watch the kites in the sky."	Senses: sight, touch, taste Mood: happy, contented

Teaching Chess, and Life
Feeding Frenzy

Reading Skill: Using Sources

In doing research, you will find two basic types of sources. A **primary source** is a firsthand account, often using first-person pronouns like *I* and *me*. Examples are autobiographies, interviews, oral histories, essays, and speeches. A **secondary source** is a secondhand account, often using third-person pronouns like *he, she,* and *they.* Examples are encyclopedias, textbooks, biographies, and many newspaper articles.

To get the most out of primary and secondary sources:

- **Analyze.** Decide whether the work is a primary or secondary source. Then, look for the **main idea.** Ask yourself, "How well does the author support the main idea?" "What is the author's purpose in writing the work?" and "Who is the author's audience?"

- **Evaluate.** Look for clues that tell you whether the author is presenting **facts** or **opinions.** Are the facts accurate? Do you agree with the author's opinions?

- **Elaborate.** When you elaborate, you add information. You might present your own ideas or do additional research.

Into the Articles

The selections you are about to read are what journalists call human-interest stories. The first selection, "Teaching Chess, and Life," is a firsthand account of how a teacher used the game of chess to change a boy's life. "Feeding Frenzy" is a secondhand account of a boy who started a food-sharing program.

Teaching Chess, and Life

BASED ON THE ARTICLES

FROM **The New York Times,** September 3, 2000

Carlos Capellan

FEEDING FRENZY

FROM **People,** June 2, 1997

Peter Ames Carlin and Don Sider

Here's
HOW

USING SOURCES

Right away I can tell that this is a primary source. The first four sentences include personal experiences of the writer. The very first word, the pronoun *I*, lets me know that this is a firsthand account.

Your
TURN

USING SOURCES

One way to get the most out of your sources is to elaborate. Have you ever helped or taught a younger person? How was your experience the same as or different from that of Carlos?

_____

_____

_____

_____

_____

_____

_____

Your
TURN

USING SOURCES

How would you evaluate the impact of Chia on Carlos's life?

_____

_____

_____

_____

Teaching Chess, and Life

based on *The New York Times* article, September 3, 2000
by Carlos Capellan

I live on West 160th Street in Washington Heights.[1] Drug dealers are common here. So are people too scared to sit on their front steps. Here parents pick up their children at school and hurry off before trouble starts. This is my block and my neighborhood.

5   Many neighborhood kids my age wind up in gangs. Some deal drugs. They go to jail or die young. I decided long ago that I wouldn't end up that way. One person who helped me is my former social studies teacher and chess coach, Jeremy Chiappetta.

    Once I was playing chess for a top prize. It was the last round,
10 and I expected to win. Excited, I began to slam the pieces. Chia's[2] big hand stopped the game clock. We talked about sportsmanship. I apologized to my opponent and gave up my win. I didn't get a prize.

    Later, I had to teach the same lesson to others when I helped Chia with a chess team at Intermediate School 90. The kids learned
15 the game Chia had taught me to love.

    Before Chia left I.S.[3] 90, he recommended that I become an assistant chess coach—with pay. I now teach chess three days a week. I also watch and help the team at contests on weekends.

    Mr. Chiappetta made this possible. He kept me involved with
20 chess. Chess kept me off the streets. It's taught me to think in new ways. Chess has made me a mentor for younger students. It's given me the chance to become their Chia.

---

1. **Washington Heights:** neighborhood in New York City.
2. **Chia:** shortened version of "Chiappetta"; a nickname for the chess coach.
3. **I.S.:** abbreviation of "Intermediate School."

Feeding Frenzy

based on the *People* article, June 2, 1997

by Peter Ames Carlin and Don Sider

Fifteen-year-old David Levitt works every week at the Haven of Rest food bank.[1] People there think he's a good Samaritan.[2]

At the age of eleven, Levitt designed a food-sharing program. Since 1994, the program has sent food to the shelters and food

5 banks of Pinellas County, Florida. The hungry have received more than a quarter-million pounds of leftover food. The extra food comes from public-school cafeterias. Levitt is now backing a state law to protect donors of surplus food from liability lawsuits.[3]

Levitt got the idea for his food program in 1993. He had read

10 about a nonprofit group called Kentucky Harvest. It sends leftover food from restaurants to groups that help poor people. Levitt learned that 30 million people in this country often go to bed hungry, yet nearly 20 percent of usable food is thrown away. Levitt asked his principal for permission to start a Harvest program. The program

15 would use cafeteria leftovers.

The principal pointed out that health laws ban using previously served food. Encouraged by his mother, Levitt took his food plan for a local Harvest program to the school board. He won its approval and its applause.

20 Next, Levitt had to face the rules of the state health department. He needed special bags that the school could not afford. Levitt got help from a major corporation. It promptly shipped him eight cases of plastic bags. On November 9, 1994, Levitt made his first delivery of school food to Haven of Rest.

---

1. **food bank:** a central facility that supplies food to charity groups. The groups then give food to people who need it.
2. **good Samaritan:** a person who unselfishly helps others. The term comes from a Bible story (Luke 10:30–37).
3. **liability lawsuits:** legal actions brought against a person or group to make up for loss or damage that has occurred.

From "Feeding Frenzy" by Peter Ames Carlin and Don Sider adapted from *People Magazine*, June 2, 1997, pp. 101–102. Copyright © 1997 by **People Weekly**. Retold by Holt, Rinehart and Winston. All rights reserved. Reproduced by permission of the publisher.

USING SOURCES

In the first two lines, I can tell that this is a secondhand account. The writer uses the pronoun *he*, so the story must be a summary of someone else's experience. I remember that a secondhand account is a secondary source.

Your
TURN

USING SOURCES

If you evaluate lines 1–8, you'll discover that most of the statements are facts. Circle the one opinion.

Your
TURN

USING SOURCES

Elaborate on this source by describing any activity you know that kids in your school do to help others.

_____

_____

_____

_____

_____

_____

_____

_____

_____

_____

25   Levitt gets A's and B's in school. He plays volleyball and a few musical instruments. He thinks about attending the U.S. Air Force Academy. He says, "Call me tomorrow—I might change."

What doesn't change is Levitt's ability to make things happen. He's lucky to have a mother who helps push his projects along. His
30 energy has won him plenty of fans. One fan is Stan Curtis, who started the first Harvest program. Curtis says, "Any parent in America would be glad to have him as a son."

Former president William J. Clinton awarded Levitt a medal from the Points of Light Foundation. The foundation honors people for
35 outstanding community service. When he received the medal, Levitt asked, "What do you do with the White House leftovers?"

Using Sources

When you research a subject, you use two kinds of sources: primary and secondary sources. A **primary source** is a firsthand account of an event. It includes the experiences, opinions, and ideas of the speaker. A **secondary source** is a secondhand account of an event. It includes summaries, interpretations, and analyses of events in which the speaker did not participate.

The list below contains sources that you might use to research an annual music festival. Identify each source as primary or secondary by placing a check mark in the correct box. One item is done for you.

Source	Primary or Secondary?
1. A television interview with a musician at the music festival	Primary ☐ Secondary ☐
2. Chapter of a biography on the founder of the music festival	Primary ☐ Secondary ☐
3. Newspaper editorial about the music festival	Primary ☐ Secondary ☑
4. Written version of a welcome speech given by the festival's chairman at this year's festival	Primary ☐ Secondary ☐
5. Information on the festival from the Chamber of Commerce	Primary ☐ Secondary ☐
6. An encyclopedia article on music festivals around the world	Primary ☐ Secondary ☐

Marigolds

Literary Focus: External and Internal Conflict

At the heart of a story is **conflict,** or struggle. When characters struggle against something outside themselves, the conflict is **external.** Characters with **internal conflict** struggle against opposing desires or personal problems such a fear, anger, or shyness. "Marigolds" includes a violent external conflict and internal conflicts in Lizabeth.

EXTERNAL CONFLICT

I want to play ball, but I need to do research for my report.

INTERNAL CONFLICT

Reading Skill: Making Inferences About Motivation

When you wonder why characters behave as they do, you are trying to figure out their **motivation.** Writers often don't make direct statements about their characters. You have to make **inferences,** or educated guesses, based on your own prior knowledge and the details in the text.

Into the Story

"Marigolds" is set in a small town in Maryland during the Great Depression of the 1930s. During this time many people lost their jobs and their savings. Businesses and factories closed down all over America. The narrator says that for poor families like hers, the Depression was nothing new.

Marigolds

BASED ON THE STORY BY
Eugenia W. Collier

I remember my childhood hometown as dusty. The dust got into the eyes and throat and between the toes of bare brown feet. Although there must have been green lawns and paved streets somewhere in town, I remember things not as they were, but as they *felt*. I
5 remember only the dirt of the shantytown where I lived and one bright splash of sunny yellow, Miss Lottie's marigolds.

Whenever I think of those marigolds, I feel a strange longing for the past that lasts even after the picture has faded. I again know the confused feelings of a teenager. Joy, anger, animal gladness and
10 shame tangle together as I think about fourteen-going-on-fifteen. I remember becoming more woman than child. That was years ago in Miss Lottie's yard.

The Depression was no new thing to us. Black farm workers had always been poor, so I don't know what we were waiting
15 for—not the good times "just around the corner." Those were white folks' words that we never believed. We didn't wait for hard work to pay off, and we didn't count on the American Dream. Perhaps we waited for a miracle, but God wasn't passing out miracles in those days. So we waited—and waited.

20 We children didn't know how poor we were. We had no radios, few newspapers, and no magazines to tie us to the outside world. Everybody we knew was hungry and poorly dressed. We were trapped in the cage of poverty.

As I think of those days, I feel most sad remembering the
25 end of those summers. That was a bright, dry time when we began to notice the days were getting shorter and the cold was on its way.

That summer Joey and I were the only children at home. The older ones had married or moved to the city. The two babies had
30 been sent away to family members. Joey, who was three years younger than I and a boy, was, therefore, inferior. Mother went to her maid's job, and Father looked for work. After doing our chores, Joey and I were free to run wild in the sun with other children.

"Marigolds" by **Eugenia W. Collier** adapted from *Negro Digest*, November 1969. Copyright © 1969 by Johnson Publishing Company, Inc. Retold by Holt, Rinehart and Winston. Reproduced by permission of the author.

Most of those days run together in my memory. I felt something
35 old and familiar was ending. Something unknown and scary was
beginning.

One day comes back to me most clearly. My loss of innocence
began that day. I was daydreaming under our great oak tree. Joey
was with his friends. He yelled, "Hey, Lizabeth. Let's go
40 somewhere."

"Where you want to go? What you want to do?"

We'd tired of our shapeless summer days. In the spring we
looked forward to freedom. Now it bored us. We needed to fill the
empty midday hours.

45 Joey's eyes shone. "Let's go to Miss Lottie's," he said.

The idea caught on. We loved to tease Miss Lottie. We were
five or six kids of different ages. We each wore only one piece of
clothing. The girls were in too long or too short dresses, and the
boys wore patched pants, their sweaty brown chests bare.

50 The sun and rain had turned Miss Lottie's house from white to
gray. The boards seemed to just lean together without nails, like a
child's house of cards. A sharp wind might have blown it down. It
stood on a lot with no grass, not even weeds.

Miss Lottie's son, John Burke, who sat in a squeaky rocking
55 chair, was known as strange. Black and ageless, he rocked all the
time. Usually he lived in his quiet dream world, but if you bothered
him, he'd be angry. We children made a game of bothering him.

But Miss Lottie was our real fun and our real fear. She seemed
to be a hundred years old. She'd once been a tall, powerful woman.
60 Now she was bent and drawn. Her smooth skin was a dark reddish
brown, and her calm face, like our idea of Indian faces, showed no
sign of joy or pain. She didn't like trespassers, especially children.
She never left her yard, and nobody ever visited her. We'd once
thought she was a witch, and we'd half believed the stories we made
65 up about her. We no longer believed the witch nonsense, but old fears
cling like cobwebs. We had to stop and get up our nerve as we neared
her yard.

"Look, there she is," I whispered, forgetting she couldn't hear
me from so far away. "She's fooling with them crazy flowers."
70 "Yeh, look at her."

Your TURN

MAKING INFERENCES ABOUT MOTIVATION

The children in the story love to tease Miss Lottie (line 46). Why do they like to pick on her? Underline clues in the text in lines 58–67. Then, write your answer on the lines below.

_____
_____
_____
_____
_____
_____
_____
_____
_____
_____
_____
_____
_____
_____

Here's HOW

VOCABULARY

I've seen "No Trespassing" signs before. I know that means you can't go on that property. So I'm pretty sure *trespassers* in line 62 means "people who go on someone's property without permission."

Here's
HOW

**EXTERNAL AND
INTERNAL CONFLICT**

In lines 82–85, I see internal
conflict in the narrator as a
teenage girl. She wants to join
the fun, but maybe she thinks
she's too old for this cruel joke.

Your
TURN

**MAKING INFERENCES
ABOUT MOTIVATION**

Lizabeth hesitates in teasing
Miss Lottie (lines 84–85).
What makes her decide to
join in (lines 86–88)?

_____

_____

_____

_____

_____

_____

Your
TURN

**EXTERNAL AND
INTERNAL CONFLICT**

Is the battle between the
children and Miss Lottie an
external or an internal conflict?

_____

_____

_____

Her marigolds didn't fit with the house and yard. They were a bright strip of blossoms. They clumped together in huge mounds. They were warm and sun golden. The old black witch-woman worked on them all summer while the house crumbled and John Burke
75 rocked.

We children hated those marigolds. They didn't fit in with the ugly place. They were too beautiful. They said something we could not understand. They made no sense. We had to tease her. We threw small stones into her flowers and yelled a dirty word and
80 danced away. We really wanted to destroy her flowers, but nobody had the nerve, not even Joey and he'd try most anything.

"Y'all git some stones," ordered Joey now. Everyone except me gathered stones. "Come on, Lizabeth."

I stood staring through the bushes. I wanted to join the fun, but
85 I also felt it was a bit silly.

"You scared, Lizabeth?"

"Y'all children get the stones," I said. "I'll show you how to use them."

Miss Lottie worked calmly, kneeling over the flowers. Her dark
90 hand was hidden in the golden mound. Suddenly *zing*—a perfectly aimed stone cut off the head of a blossom.

"Who out there?" Her sharp eyes searched the bushes. "You better git!"

We hid in the bushes as Miss Lottie looked across the road.
95 Then she returned to her weeding. *Zing*—Joey sent a stone into the blooms, and another marigold was beheaded.

Miss Lottie was angry now. She rose slowly to her feet, leaning on a cane and shouting. "Y'all git! Go on home!" But the children didn't stop throwing stones and laughing. She shook her stick at us,
100 crying, "Git along! John Burke, come help!"

Then, mad with power, I lost my head. I went toward Miss Lottie, chanting madly. "Old witch fell in a ditch, picked up a penny and thought she was rich!" The children screamed with delight. They dropped their stones and danced crazily. We swarmed about
105 Miss Lottie like bees. We chanted, "Old lady witch!" She screamed curses at us. The madness lasted only a moment as John Burke,

startled at last, left his chair while we dashed for cover. Miss Lottie's cane flew at my head.

I didn't join the fun under the oak in our backyard. Suddenly I was ashamed, and I didn't like the feeling. The child in me said it was in fun, but the woman in me flinched at the thought of the mean attack I had led.

I awoke in the night to voices. At first I heard no words, only voices, through the thin walls. My mother's voice was peaceful, quiet, but my father's voice destroyed the peace.

"Twenty-two years, Maybelle," he said. "And I got nothing for you, nothing, nothing."

"It's all right, honey. You'll get something. Everybody out of work now. You know that."

"It aint right. Ain't no man ought to eat his woman's food. See his children running wild."

"Honey, you took good care of us when you could. Ain't nobody got nothing nowadays."

"I ain't talking about nobody else. I'm talking about me."

"We ain't starving. Miss Ellis pay me every week. She'll give you Mr. Ellis's old coat."

"You think I want white folks' leavings?" He sobbed loudly. I'd never heard a man cry before. I didn't know men ever cried. I covered my ears with my hands. Finally it quieted. My mother hummed softly as she did for scared children.

Everything was suddenly out of tune. Where did I fit into this crazy picture? I felt great fear. Finally, feeling the terrible aloneness of 4 A.M., I woke Joey.

"Come on, wake up."

"What for? Go away."

I couldn't answer. So I said, "I'm going out. If you want to come, come on."

The promise of adventure woke him. "Going out now? Where to, Lizabeth? What you going to do?"

I was out the window and down the road before he caught up. Somewhat surprised, I reached Miss Lottie's yard.

EXTERNAL AND INTERNAL CONFLICT

What is causing the narrator's internal conflict in lines 109–112?

_____

_____

_____

VOCABULARY

Go back to line 111. What do you think the word *flinched* means?

_____

_____

MAKING INFERENCES ABOUT MOTIVATION

Why do you think Lizabeth feels great fear when she hears her father crying?

_____

_____

_____

_____

_____

_____

EXTERNAL AND INTERNAL CONFLICT

In lines 143–146, underline Lizabeth's internal conflicts. What external conflict does she engage in to express her internal conflicts?

_____

_____

_____

_____

MAKING INFERENCES ABOUT MOTIVATION

Why do you think Lizabeth's destructive act led her to finally feel compassion, or sympathy, for another human being?

_____

_____

_____

_____

_____

_____

_____

_____

_____

_____

_____

_____

_____

"Lizabeth, you lost your mind?" panted Joey.

I had indeed lost my mind. My emotions swelled up in me and burst—the need for my mother who was never there, the
145 hopelessness of our poverty, the confusion of being neither child nor woman, the fear caused by my father's tears. These feelings led to an urge for destruction. I leaped into the marigolds and pulled madly. I destroyed the perfect yellow blooms. Finally I sat in the ruined garden and cried and cried. It was too late to undo anything. Joey sat beside
150 me, silent and frightened.

I saw a pair of large callused feet and an aged body in a cotton nightdress. No anger showed in the face now. Now that the garden was destroyed, there was nothing to protect.

"Miss Lottie!" I stared at her as childhood faded and
155 womanhood began. I stared at sad, tired eyes. I saw a truth children miss. The witch was no longer a witch. She was a broken old woman. She'd dared to create beauty from ugliness.

I couldn't explain what I knew about Miss Lottie then, as I stood there ashamed. But years have put words in my mouth. In that
160 moment I saw past myself. I looked deep into another person. That was the end of innocence and the beginning of compassion.

Time has taken me far from that place. Miss Lottie died long ago. She never planted marigolds again. Yet, still I see those yellow mounds. One does not have to be poor to find life empty, as empty as
165 those dusty yards. And I too have planted marigolds.

External and Internal Conflict

We see an **external conflict** in "Marigolds" as Lizabeth and her friends destroy an old woman's garden. However, the main conflicts in the story are inside the mind and heart of Lizabeth. In **internal conflict,** a character struggles with a personal problem, such as fear, shyness, anger, or anxiety.

What causes Lizabeth's internal conflicts? Fill out the chart below to explore how Lizabeth reacts to and copes with the challenges listed. One item has been done for you.

Challenge	Lizabeth's Feelings
1. family's poverty	At the beginning of the story, the narrator says the children didn't know they were poor. But hearing her father cry about not having a job seemed to make her afraid and confused. I think that's why she destroyed the marigolds.
2. relationship with Joey and the other children	
3. becoming a woman	
4. beauty of the marigolds	

The Interlopers

Literary Focus: Surprise Ending

A great **surprise ending** is one that makes sense but that you probably did not predict. In Saki's story the surprise at the end makes readers rethink the entire story. The surprise gives new meaning to the events that happened before it and leads readers to the author's message.

Reading Skill: Monitoring Your Reading

Good readers have learned to monitor their reading. They know when to seek help and what strategies to use to get through a tough passage. See how good you are at monitoring your reading of Saki's unusual story. Here is how to monitor your reading:

- Ask questions. Make predictions as you read.
- When you don't understand a word, and it is not defined, look for context clues.
- Break down long sentences into simpler sentences.
- Look for the subject and verb in complicated sentences.
- Stop at the end of a passage you think is important, and retell it in your own words. If you haven't understood the passage, re-read it.

Into the Story

This story is set in a thick forest on the slopes of the Carpathian (kahr PAY thee uhn) Mountains. These mountains stretch through Poland, Slovakia, Romania, and Ukraine. The story is set around the end of the nineteenth century. At this time, wealthy, noble families owned miles and miles of land—almost entire countries.

A poacher is someone who goes onto private property to fish or hunt illegally. In Europe at one time, someone caught poaching could be put to death.

BASED ON THE STORY BY
Saki

The Interlopers

Here's HOW

MONITORING YOUR READING

I've re-read the first two paragraphs. I see that two families have been fighting over the same piece of land for years. I predict this struggle will be important to the story.

Your TURN

MONITORING YOUR READING

Ulrich guesses what is disturbing the animals (line 20). What do you think is disturbing them?

_____

_____

_____

_____

Here's HOW

VOCABULARY

I see in lines 21–22 that Ulrich is searching for poachers. I remember reading on page 30 that poachers are people who hunt or fish without permission on someone else's land.

A man stood watching and listening one winter night in a dark forest on the eastern side of the Carpathian Mountains. He acted as if he were hunting game. But this man was hunting a different sort of animal. Ulrich von Gradwitz[1] was searching for a human enemy.

His family's large forestland was full of game; however, few animals could be found where Ulrich waited. Still, Ulrich guarded this land jealously. In a famous lawsuit during the days of his grandfather, his family had won back the land from a neighboring family. The losing family had no legal claim to the land, but still they had never accepted the court's ruling. For three generations now, the two families had been enemies.

Now that Ulrich was the head of his family, the fighting had become personal. Ulrich detested Georg Znaeym,[2] his warring neighbor. Georg went on killing game in Ulrich's forest. The feud continued because the two men hated each other so much.

On this windy winter night, Ulrich had ordered his servants to watch for thieves in the forest.

All the animals in the forest usually hid in safe places in bad weather, but tonight they were restless. Something was upsetting the forest and the animals that night. Ulrich could guess what it was.

He had his watchers hiding on the hilltop. Then he wandered alone listening through the wild, whistling wind for poachers. His greatest wish was to come face to face with Georg Znaeym, to meet him alone. As he stepped around a huge tree trunk, he met Georg.

The two enemies glared at each other for a long moment. Each held a rifle, and each had hate in his heart and murder on his mind. Finally, they had the chance of a lifetime, but neither could just shoot a man in cold blood without a word spoken.

Before either could act, a fierce wind blew against the massive tree over their heads. With a splitting crash, the tree thundered down upon them. Ulrich found himself on the ground with one arm numb beneath him, the other arm caught in the branches, and both legs pinned beneath the trunk. Twigs had slashed his face, causing him to blink blood from his eyelashes in order to see. Georg lay close by his side. He was alive and struggling, pinned down like Ulrich.

---

1. **Ulrich von Gradwitz** (UHL rihk fahn GRAHT vihts).
2. **Georg Znaeym** (jawrj ZNY uhm).

Ulrich was glad to be alive, but he was angry at being trapped. He mumbled a strange mixture of thanks and sharp curses.

"So you're not dead, but you're caught anyway," Georg cried. "What a joke! Ulrich von Gradwitz caught in his stolen forest!"

40 "I'm caught in my own forest," Ulrich replied. "My men will free me soon. Then you'll wish you hadn't been caught stealing game."

Georg was silent a moment, then answered quietly: "Are you sure your men will find much to release? I have men, too. They're in the forest tonight, close behind me. *They* will be here first. When they 45 drag me out from under these branches, it won't take much clumsiness on their part to roll this trunk on top of you. Your men will find you dead under a fallen tree. I'll send condolences to let your family know how sorry I am."

"That's a useful plan," said Ulrich fiercely. "My men had orders to 50 follow in ten minutes, and seven minutes must have passed already. When they get me out, I'll remember that plan. But since you will have met your death while poaching on my land, I don't think I can decently send any condolences to your family."

"Good," snarled Georg. "You and I and our men will fight this to 55 the death, with no interfering outsiders here."

Both men knew that they might be defeated or found too late. Which team would get there first was a matter of chance.

Both stopped struggling to get free. Ulrich managed to get his wine flask[3] from his pocket. Though it was a mild winter and Ulrich 60 felt the cold less than he might have, the drink warmed and revived the wounded man. He looked over at Georg with a throb of pity.

"Could you reach this flask if I tossed it to you?" asked Ulrich suddenly. "There is good wine in it. We may as well be as comfortable as we can."

65 "No. I can't see to catch it," said Georg. "Anyway, I don't drink with an enemy."

Ulrich was silent for a few minutes. An idea was slowly forming in him, an idea that gained strength every time he looked at Georg. In his pain and weariness, the old hatred seemed to be dying.

---

3. **flask:** a flat container that fits in a pocket. A flask typically holds alcohol.

VOCABULARY

I'm not sure what the word *condolences* means in line 47. I think it means "messages of sorrow" because the next line says "how sorry I am."

SURPRISE ENDING

I know that this story has a surprise ending. Lines 54–55 suggest the two men will fight until one of them dies, but that would not be a surprise to me. So, the story will probably end in another way.

MONITORING YOUR READING

In lines 67–68, what do you think is Ulrich's idea? Make a prediction about it on the lines below.

_____

_____

_____

_____

_____

_____

_____

70 "Neighbor," he said, "do what you like if your men come first. But, I've changed my mind. If my men come first, they will help you first. We have fought like devils over this stupid forest. I see we've been fools. If you'll help me end this fight, we can be friends."

After a silence, Georg finally spoke. "Think how people would 75 stare if we rode into the market square together! No one living can remember our families being friendly. And if we choose to make peace, there is none other to interfere, no interlopers from outside. I never thought of anything but hating you. But I think I've changed my mind, too. Ulrich von Gradwitz, I will be your friend."

80 For a time, both men thought about the wonderful changes peace would bring. In the cold, gloomy forest on that windy night, they lay and waited for help. Each prayed that his men would arrive first. Then, he might be the first to help his new friend.

Soon, the wind died down. Ulrich said, "Let's shout for help."

85 "Our voices won't carry far," said Georg, "but we can try. Together, then."

The two men cried out.

"Together again," said Ulrich after waiting a few minutes. Then he said, "I heard something that time, I think."

90 "I heard nothing but the cursed wind," said Georg.

After a few minutes of silence, Ulrich gave a joyful cry.

"I can see figures coming through the wood."

Both men shouted as loudly as they could.

"They hear us! They're running down the hill toward us," cried 95 Ulrich.

"How many of them are there?" asked Georg.

"I can't see clearly. Nine or ten," said Ulrich.

"Then they are yours," said Georg. "I had only seven men."

"They are hurrying as fast as they can," said Ulrich gladly.

100 "Are they your men?" asked Georg. "Are they your men?" he repeated impatiently, as Ulrich did not answer.

"No," said Ulrich with a strange laugh. It was the idiotic, chattering laugh of a man full of hideous fear.

"Who are they?" asked Georg, straining his eyes to see what the 105 other man wished he had not seen.

"Wolves."

Surprise Ending

A surprise ending is one you did not predict but makes sense anyway. A surprise ending is a powerful way of suggesting an author's basic message about human nature and people's behavior. The ending of "The Interlopers" is especially powerful because the reader and the characters don't expect it. The ending also suggests the author's message about life.

Fill out the following graphic organizer in order to explore the surprise ending of "The Interlopers." One section has been done for you.

EXPLAIN

Why did the ending surprise you?

I thought there would be

a happy ending when the

former enemies became

friends.

GUESS

What do you think happens to the men in the end?

_____

_____

_____

ANALYZE

How is the ending related to the story's message?

_____

_____

_____

The Necklace

Literary Focus: Third-Person-Limited Point of View

In some stories told from the third-person point of view (stories using the pronouns *he, she,* and *they*), you learn the thoughts and feelings of all the characters. Stories told from the **third-person-limited point of view,** however, focus on the thoughts and feelings of only one character. The story of "The Necklace" is mostly told from the point of view of a French housewife, Mathilde Loisel.

Third-Person-Limited Point of View

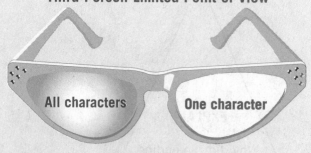

All characters   One character

Reading Skill: Summarizing

You can summarize many stories by using this simple sentence: Somebody wants _____, but _____, so _____. For example, Cinderella *wants* to go to the ball, *but* she has nothing to wear, *so* her fairy godmother gives her fine clothes and a handsome carriage. Keep this formula in mind as you read "The Necklace." Then, after you finish the story, try to summarize the plot by filling in the blanks in the sentence above. You will have to repeat the sentence to summarize the whole story.

Into the Story

The setting for "The Necklace" is Paris in the 1880s. In France at that time, there was a strict division of classes. The wealthy lived in comfort and luxury, but life was more difficult for the poor and middle classes. In "The Necklace" a young middle-class woman yearns for all the pleasures wealth brings. This desire has tragic results for her husband and herself.

The Necklace

BASED ON THE STORY BY

Guy de Maupassant

Here's HOW

VOCABULARY

The word *dowry* in line 2 is new to me. I can tell what it means, though, by reading the words that follow it.

Here's HOW

POINT OF VIEW

The first sentence tells me exactly who is the focus of this story. In lines 5–6, I learn that Mathilde is unhappy. She dreams about being rich.

Here's HOW

SUMMARIZING

I'll summarize lines 14–33: *Somebody* (Mathilde) wants to look beautiful at the party, *but* she doesn't have the right clothes, *so* her husband gives her money for a new gown.

Mathilde[1] was a pretty, charming, middle-class girl. She had no dowry—no money from her family to take to her marriage—and no way to meet a rich man, so she married a clerk in the Ministry of Education.

5   She dressed plainly, but she was unhappy because she couldn't afford fine clothes. She daydreamed about being rich.

    At dinner her husband would say, "Ah! A good stew! There's nothing I like better. . . ." She'd dream of fancy dinner parties.

    She had no evening clothes or jewelry, but she wanted them and 10 felt she should have them. She longed to be envied and desired.

    One evening her husband handed her an invitation. Excited, she opened it and found an invitation to a grand party at the Ministerial Mansion.

    She tossed it aside, saying, "What good is that to me?"

15   "I thought you'd be thrilled since you never get to go out. I had an awful time getting invited. Everybody wants to go, but few clerks can. The most important people will be there."

    She gave him a sour look and cried, "What do you think I would wear?"

20   He hadn't thought about that. "Why, the dress you wear to the theater. That looks quite nice."

    He was surprised when she burst into tears. He gasped, "Why, what's the matter?" Using all her willpower, she stopped crying. "Oh, nothing. I don't have an evening gown, so I can't go to that party."

25   He was stunned. He said, "How much would the right outfit cost? Something simple?"

    She thought it over for several seconds. She thought of her allowance and about how much her husband might give her.

    Finally, she answered, "I'm not sure exactly. Maybe I could 30 manage with four hundred francs."[2]

    He turned pale because he'd saved that much for a rifle and planned to go hunting with friends.

---

1. **Mathilde** (mah TIHLD).
2. **francs:** French money.

However, he said, "All right. I'll give you four hundred francs."

As the party neared, Mme. Loisel[3] seemed sad. She was moody
35 and upset although her outfit was ready. One evening her husband
asked, "What's the matter?"

She answered, "I'm embarrassed not to have any jewelry."

Her husband said, "Borrow some from your rich friend Mme.
Forestier.[4] You're good enough friends to do that."

40 She said, "Why didn't I think of that!"

The next day she went to her friend, who offered her a large
jewelry box. "Pick out something, my dear."

Mathilde found a diamond necklace. Her heart beat faster, and her
hands shook when she picked it up. "Could I borrow this one?" she
45 asked.

"Why, of course."

She hugged her friend, kissed her warmly, and fled with her prize.

Mme. Loisel was a hit at the party. The prettiest one there, she
was stylish, warm, smiling, and wildly happy. All the men turned to
50 look at her. They asked who she was and begged to meet her. The
Cabinet members waltzed with her, and the minister noticed her.

She danced madly, wildly, drunk with joy. Around four o'clock the
Loisels took a shabby cab home. For her, it was all over, but he had to
face the office at ten o'clock.

55 She looked at herself in the mirror one last time. The necklace
was gone! She cried out.

Her husband, already half undressed, said, "What's wrong?"

Upset, she turned toward him. "I . . . I . . . I don't have my
friend's necklace."

60 "That's impossible." They hunted everywhere in the apartment
but found nothing. He retraced their steps, searching for hours. She
slumped in a chair in the cold room.

Her husband came in around seven o'clock. He'd had no luck
finding the necklace.

65 By the end of the week, they had given up all hope. Loisel looked
five years older. He said, "We must replace the necklace."

---

3. **Mme. Loisel** (mah DAHM lwah ZEHL): *Mme.* is an abbreviation of "Madame," the French
   equivalent of *Mrs.*
4. **Forestier** (faw ruhs TYAY).

Your TURN

POINT OF VIEW

Re-read lines 34–36. Circle
Mathilde's thoughts and
feelings in these sentences.

Your TURN

SUMMARIZING

Somebody (Mathilde) wants
jewelry to go with her new
gown, *but* she can't afford any,
so _____. Re-read
lines 41–47, and then describe
how she overcomes this
difficulty.

_____

_____

_____

_____

_____

Here's HOW

SUMMARIZING

Somebody (Mathilde) wants to
admire her outfit one last time,
but the necklace is missing, *so*
her husband spends hours
searching for it.

They found a necklace exactly like the first. It cost forty thousand francs, but they could get it for thirty-six.

Loisel had eighteen thousand francs he had inherited from his
70 father. He borrowed the rest. He got a thousand francs from one, four hundred from another—a hundred here, sixty there. He signed notes, made deals with loan sharks, borrowed from moneylenders.

When Mme. Loisel returned the necklace, her friend said coldly, "You should have returned it sooner. I might have needed it."
75 Mme. Forestier didn't open the case.

Mme. Loisel bravely faced being poor. That debt had to be paid, and she would pay it. She let her maid go, and she and her husband moved to a cheap attic apartment.

She cooked and did housework. She scrubbed the laundry, hung it
80 on a line to dry, took out the garbage, carried up water, and dressed like a peasant. She watched every coin she spent. She bargained for food with the fruit dealer, the grocer, and the butcher, and they insulted her.

Her husband worked evenings as a bookkeeper, and at night he
85 copied documents for five sous[5] a page.

This lasted for ten years.

Finally, all the debts and interest were paid.

Mme. Loisel looked like an old woman now. Sometimes she'd remember when she had been so beautiful and admired.
90 What if she hadn't lost the necklace? Who knows? How little there is between joy and misery!

Then one Sunday, she went for a walk. She saw a woman strolling with a child. It was Mme. Forestier. She still looked young and beautiful.
95 Mme. Loisel went toward her friend saying, "Hello, Jeanne."

The other was surprised to be spoken to so familiarly. "But . . . madame . . . I don't recognize . . . You must be mistaken."

"No, I'm Mathilde Loisel."

Her friend cried out, "Oh, my poor Mathilde! How you're
100 changed!"

---

5. **sous:** plural of *sou,* an old French coin of little value.

"Yes, I've had a hard time. And plenty of problems—and all because of you!"

"Of me . . . what do you mean?" Mme. Forestier asked.

"Do you remember the diamond necklace I borrowed?"

105 "Yes. What about it?"

"I lost it," Mathilde said.

"But you returned it."

"I bought another just like it, and we have been paying for it for ten years. Well, it's over now, and I am glad."

110 Mme. Forestier was surprised. "You bought a diamond necklace to replace mine!"

"Yes. You never noticed, then? They were quite alike." Mathilde smiled with proud and simple joy.

Mme. Forestier, quite overcome, clasped her by the hands. "Oh,
115 my poor Mathilde. Mine was fake. Why, at most it was worth only five hundred francs!"

Here's HOW

POINT OF VIEW

I know that Mathilde and her husband worked hard to pay for the necklace. I learn something new about Mathilde's feelings in lines 112–113. I see that she is proud and even joyful that her friend never knew her original necklace was lost.

Your TURN

POINT OF VIEW

The plot comes to a sudden stop in lines 114–116. Underline the short sentence that changes the whole story. How might this new information change Mathilde's feelings about her life and her sacrifices?

_____

_____

_____

_____

_____

_____

_____

_____

_____

_____

_____

_____

_____

Third-Person-Limited Point of View

A story's **point of view** is the vantage point from which the story is told. When a narrator who is not a character in the story focuses on one character, the story is told from the **third-person-limited point of view.** In "The Necklace" the author uses this point of view to help us zoom in on Mathilde and learn her thoughts and feelings.

Re-read lines 1–49. Then, fill out the chart below to explore what you learned about Mathilde. One answer is provided for you.

Focus on Mathilde Loisel
What do we learn about
a. her past?   We learn in the story that Mathilde comes from a middle-class family and has no dowry.
b. her present?
c. what makes her unhappy?
d. what she thinks will make her happy?

Summarizing

The plot of many stories can be summed up with this simple sentence: **Somebody wants** . . . , **but** . . . , **so** . . . The formula may repeat itself several times in the story, and it may involve several different characters. The plot begins with **somebody** (the character) who **wants** something badly, **but** something or someone stands in the way (the conflict), **so** the character takes action to overcome the obstacle.

In the chart below, fill in the blanks of the sentence—two times for Mathilde and two times for her husband. One item is completed for you.

Somebody (Mathilde)	Somebody (Mathilde's husband)
1. wants ...	3. wants ... a new hunting rifle
but ...	but ...
so ...	so ...
2. wants ...	4. wants ...
but ...	but ...
so ...	so ...

The Cask of Amontillado

Literary Focus: Unreliable Narrator

When you read, you usually believe the narrator who is telling the story. However, some stories have an **unreliable narrator**—a narrator you cannot trust. Over the years since Poe wrote this story, people have asked whether the narrator is telling the truth or telling lies. Once you finish the story, ask yourself whether you trust the narrator.

Reading Skill: Drawing Conclusions

When you **draw conclusions,** you pay attention to details in the text. Then you combine those details with your own knowledge to form a new idea about the text.

text   +   **what you know**   =   **your conclusion**

Into the Story

Centuries ago in Italy, the early Christians buried their dead in catacombs, which are winding underground tunnels. Later, wealthy families built private catacombs underneath their homes. Dark and cool, these chambers were suitable not only for burial but also for storing wine.

This story is set during carnival, a time for people to have fun before the Christian season of Lent begins. (During Lent, many people eat or drink very little and often give up meat altogether.) People celebrate carnival by eating and drinking, wearing costumes, and dancing in the streets.

The Cask of Amontillado

BASED ON THE STORY BY
Edgar Allan Poe

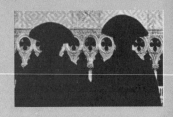

I put up with Fortunato[1] for years. When he insulted me, however, I decided to get even. I wouldn't threaten him. Instead, I would punish him without getting caught.

I went on smiling at him. He didn't guess that I was smiling at the
5 thought of his destruction.

Fortunato was a man to respect and fear. But he had a weakness: He was proud of his knowledge of wines. I plotted to use Fortunato's pride against him.

One evening during carnival I saw Fortunato. He greeted me with
10 much warmth, for he was drunk. He wore a clown costume and cone-shaped cap with jingling bells. I was very pleased to see him.

I said, "It's lucky we met. I just bought some wine. It's supposed to be amontillado."[2]

"Amontillado? To obtain such a fine wine during carnival—
15 impossible!"

"I have my doubts," I said. "Silly me, I paid the full price. I should have talked to you first, but I was afraid of losing a bargain."

"Amontillado!"

"I have my doubts," I said.
20 "Amontillado!"

"Since you're busy, I'll go to Luchesi.[3] If anyone knows wine, he does. He'll tell me—"

"Luchesi!" Fortunato snorted. "He's just a phony who pretends to know wine. Let's go to your cellars to have a taste."
25 "No. The cellars are damp; you'll catch a cold. Besides, you have other plans. Luchesi—"

"I don't have plans. Come," he insisted.

Putting on a black mask, I let him lead me to my palace.

As I expected, the servants had all gone to the carnival. Carrying
30 torches, we went down many stairs to the catacombs. The catacombs were a series of cellars that held the bones of my ancestors, the Montresors.[4] I also used the cellars to store wine.

My friend swayed as he walked; his bells jingled.

"The amontillado," he said.

---

1. **Fortunato** (fawr too NAW toh).
2. **amontillado** (uh MAHN tee YAH doh): a pale type of wine.
3. **Luchesi** (loo KEH see).
4. **Montresors** (mawn treh SAWRS).

35   "It's farther on." I said. "Look; do you see that white web-work
on the walls? It is niter, salt deposits left by the dampness. . . . How
long have you had that cough?"

     "Ugh! ugh! ugh!—ugh! ugh! ugh—It's nothing," he said.

     "Come," I said. "We'll go back. Your health is important. You are
40 rich, respected. You are happy—as I was once. Besides, there is
Luchesi—"

     "I won't die of a cough," he said.

     "True," I replied. "Here, this wine will keep you warm."

     I offered him wine from a bottle that lay in our path.

45   "I drink to the dead buried here," Fortunato said.

     "And I drink to your long life," I replied.

     "These vaults are huge," he said as we went on.

     "The Montresors were a great family," I answered.

     "I forget what your family's coat of arms is."

50   "The symbols are a human foot crushing a snake. The snake's
fangs are stuck in the heel."

     "And the motto?" he asked.

     "'Nobody attacks me without punishment,'" I replied.

     "Good!" he said.

55   We went farther into the catacombs. I paused.

     "The niter!" I said. "We're below the river. The air is *terribly*
damp. Let's return before it's too late. Your cough—!"

     "No," he said. "Let's go on. But first, more wine."

     I broke open another bottle. He emptied it in one gulp, then made
60 a strange gesture. I looked at him in surprise.

     "Aha," he said. "I see you are not a Mason."

     "Oh, yes," I said, "Yes, I am."

     "You? Impossible! Show me the secret sign," he said.

     "It is this," I answered, pulling a mason's tool from my cape.

65   "You're joking," he said, drawing back. "But let's go on."

     As we continued, our torches barely glowed in the bad air. Finally,
we entered a small chamber. Bones lined three of its walls. The bones
from the fourth wall were piled on the ground. The bare wall revealed
an opening that ended in a wall of solid rock.

70   "The amontillado is inside," I said. "As for Luchesi—"

Your TURN

UNRELIABLE NARRATOR

Re-read lines 39–41. Then, explain the narrator's hidden reason for mentioning the items below:

- Concern for Fortunato's health

_____

_____

_____

_____

- Luchesi

_____

_____

_____

_____

Here's HOW

DRAWING CONCLUSIONS

Line 61 mentions the word *Mason.* I researched this word to see what it meant. The Masons, or Freemasons, are a men's club who help each other and the poor. They use secret hand signals to recognize each other. A mason, with a small *m,* is someone who builds with stone. In lines 61–65, the word *mason* seems to be used in these two ways. I think this may be an important clue in the story.

"He's a fool," said Fortunato. He swayed into the dark opening with me behind him. Bumping into the rock wall, he stopped, confused. Quickly I chained him to the wall. He was too surprised to stop me. I stepped back.

75 "Move your hand along the wall," I said. "You'll feel the niter. It is _very_ damp. Once more let me beg you to return. No? Then I must leave you."

"The amontillado!" he cried.

"True," I replied, "the amontillado." Under the pile of bones, I

80 found building stones and cement. I began to wall up the opening.

The wine's effect was wearing off. Fortunato's moaning wasn't the cry of a drunken man. I stopped working briefly, listening with satisfaction.

Then the chained man screamed—so loudly that I became

85 worried. But feeling the thick walls of the catacomb, I became calm again. I simply screamed back, longer and louder. Fortunato's screams stopped.

Around midnight, I was almost finished. Then I heard a low laugh that made my hair stand up. It was followed by a sad voice. "Ha! ha!

90 ha!—a very good joke. We'll laugh about it later. Over our wine—he! he! he!"

"The amontillado!" I said.

"He! he! he—yes, the amontillado. But isn't it late? Lady Fortunato will be waiting for me. Let's go."

95 "Yes," I said, "Let's go."

"For the love of God, Montresor!"

"Yes," I said, "for the love of God!" He didn't answer. I called out, "Fortunato!"

No answer still. I thrust a torch through the last space in the wall

100 and let it fall inside. There came forth in return only the jingling of bells. My heart grew sick—because of the dampness. I finished sealing up the wall and piled the bones up against it. For half a century no one has bothered them. May he rest in peace.

Unreliable Narrator

An unreliable narrator can be unreliable in more than one way:

- He or she may not understand fully what is going on in the story.
- He or she may not tell us the whole truth.
- He or she may exaggerate or toy with the facts.

Poe uses an unreliable narrator to increase our sense of shock and horror. Imagine that Montresor is on trial for murder. Is Montresor guilty of coldblooded murder? Or is he not guilty by reason of insanity? There is no one correct answer, but the chart below can help you decide the verdict. One item has been done for you.

Question	Evidence from Story	Sane or Insane?
1. Is Montresor's life a sad one? Yes / No		
2. Does the amontillado really exist? Yes / (No)	Since we never see the amontillado, it likely doesn't exist. Montresor used it only as bait to pull Fortunato into the catacombs.	Sane
3. Is Montresor right about Fortunato's weakness— his pride? Yes / No		
4. Has Montresor planned Fortunato's death in great detail? Yes / No		
5. While carrying out his plan, does Montresor seem pleased or sad about what he is doing? pleased / sad		

Guilty or Not Guilty?

_____

Poe's Death Is Rewritten . . .
If Only Poe Had Succeeded . . .
Rabies Death Theory

Reading Skill: Synthesizing Sources

When you research a subject, you read many different sources, such
as Web sites and newspaper or encyclopedia articles. You then
synthesize the information, or put the pieces together to form a big
picture. To synthesize your sources:

- **Find the main ideas.** Ask yourself, "What points are the
  writers making?"
- **Look for supporting evidence,** such as facts, statistics,
  examples, anecdotes (real-life stories), and quotations.
- **Compare and contrast.** Find the similarities and differences
  in your sources.
- **Make connections.** Does the information in your sources
  remind you of anything you already know?
- **Put it all together.** You are now ready to **synthesize** what
  you've learned to form the big picture.

Into the Article and Letters

Most newspapers have what is called an Op-Ed page. The Op-Ed
page is usually found *opposite* the *editorial* page. It may include
columns by reporters who work for the paper, articles by people who
don't work for the paper, and responses to newspaper articles. These
responses are called letters to the editor. You are about to read a
newspaper article about the death of Edgar Allan Poe. Then, you will
read two letters to the editor that followed the article's publication.

BASED ON THE NEWSPAPER ARTICLE

Poe's Death Is Rewritten as Case of Rabies, Not Telltale Alcohol

FROM *The New York Times,* September 15, 1996

BASED ON THE LETTER TO THE EDITOR

If Only Poe Had Succeeded When He Said Nevermore to Drink

FROM *The New York Times,* September 23, 1996

Burton R. Pollin
Robert E. Benedetto

BASED ON THE LETTER TO THE EDITOR

Rabies Death Theory

FROM *The New York Times,* September 30, 1996

R. Michael Benitez, M.D.

Poe's Death Is Rewritten as Case of Rabies, Not Telltale Alcohol

based on the *New York Times* article, September 15, 1996

YOU NEED TO KNOW This article announced a new idea about Poe's death. Dr. R. Michael Benitez developed this idea. In the letter that follows this article, Burton R. Pollin and Robert E. Benedetto argue against Dr. Benitez's idea. Dr. Benitez responds to them in a letter defending his idea.

Dr. R. Michael Benitez claims that Edgar Allan Poe was falsely accused of drinking himself to death. The doctor says that all of Poe's symptoms point to rabies. Like many rabies victims, Poe was confused, angry, and aggressive, the doctor notes. When he was calm,
5 it was difficult for him to drink water. People with rabies often refuse or fear water because it is painful for them to swallow.

There's no evidence that a rabid animal had bitten Poe. However, rabies victims often don't remember being bitten, and the signs of rabies can take a year to show up. Once the signs appear, patients die
10 in a few days.

A doctor who treats rabies cases in Thailand agrees that Poe showed all the signs of rabies.

Because he believed that people should not drink alcohol, Poe's doctor may have changed the details of Poe's death to teach a lesson
15 about the dangers of alcohol.

Jeff Jerome, who is in charge of the Poe Baltimore House and Museum,[1] said that Poe did not die of alcohol poisoning. He said that Poe was so sensitive to alcohol that a glass of wine made him ill for days. Poe may have had problems in his youth with alcohol, but by
20 the time he was forty Poe almost always avoided alcohol, Jerome said.

---

1. **Poe Baltimore House and Museum:** a house in Baltimore, Maryland, where Poe once lived, now a museum.

"Poe's Death Is Rewritten as Case of Rabies, Not Telltale Alcohol" adapted from *The New York Times,* September 15, 1996. Copyright © 1996 by The Associated Press. Retold by Holt, Rinehart and Winston. Reproduced by permission of **The Associated Press.**

If Only Poe Had Succeeded When He Said Nevermore to Drink

based on the *New York Times* article, September 23, 1996

To the Editor:

Dr. Benitez is wrong to say that rabies, not alcoholism, caused Poe's death. Poe was found drunk and unconscious outside a bar. He died four days later. Dr. Moran's story of Poe's last days appears in a
5 letter to the woman who was both Poe's aunt and mother-in-law. Four people who saw Poe during those four days before his death—Joseph Walker, Joseph Snodgrass, and two relatives—agree that Poe was drunk. In letters to his wife and her mother, Poe wrote often about his periods of heavy drinking.

10 Dr. Benitez admits the important weakness in his idea: lack of a bite or scratch. In those days, rabies symptoms were easily recognized. If Poe had had any sign of rabies, his doctors would have seen it.

Poe's pet cat, Caterina, showed no sign of rabies. Uninfected, she
15 died of starvation after Poe's death.

There is no need to whitewash the self-destructive behavior of this genius and major American writer.

Burton R. Pollin and Robert E. Benedetto

SYNTHESIZING SOURCES

This letter to the editor gets right to the point. Read lines 1–9. Then, underline the main idea.

SYNTHESIZING SOURCES

Circle the supporting evidence for the writers' main idea.

SYNTHESIZING SOURCES

One step in synthesizing sources is to compare and contrast the sources. How are the main ideas of the article and this letter the same or different?

_____

_____

_____

_____

_____

_____

_____

_____

_____

"If Only Poe Had Succeeded When He Said Nevermore to Drink" by Burton R. Pollin adapted from "Editorial Desk" from *The New York Times*, September 23, 1996. Copyright © 1996 by **Burton R. Pollin.** Retold by Holt, Rinehart and Winston. Reproduced by permission of the author.

Rabies Death Theory

based on the *New York Times* article, September 30, 1996

To the Editor:

I do not admit that the lack of a bite or scratch is a weakness in my theory. I still say Poe may have died of rabies.

Over the past 20 years in the United States, there have been 33
5 reported cases of human rabies. Only 24 percent could recall contact with a rabid animal. Rabid bats have caused 15 cases of human rabies. Yet, only 7 patients could remember having contact with bats.

It is not easy to tell if someone has rabies. It may take as long as a year after the bite or scratch for a human to show signs of infection.
10 At Poe's death, doctors knew how rabies was passed on, but they did not yet know what caused it.

I did not suggest that Poe's cat gave him rabies. However, there was no way pets could be protected from rabies at that time.

R. Michael Benitez, M.D.

"Rabies Death Theory" by R. Michael Benitez adapted from "Editorial Desk" from *The New York Times*, Editorial Desk, September 30, 1996. Copyright © 1996 by **R. Michael Benitez.** Retold by Holt, Rinehart and Winston. Reproduced by permission of the author.

Synthesizing Sources

When you read many sources on a topic, you need to **synthesize the sources,** or fit all the pieces together into one big picture. To do that, you follow these steps: (1) find the main idea; (2) look for supporting evidence; (3) compare and contrast sources; (4) make connections; and (5) put it all together. In the chart below, fill in the boxes with the first four steps for each source. Some have been done for you. Then, synthesize the information you have gathered into one overall statement.

Article	First Letter to the Editor	Second Letter to the Editor
1. a. Main idea:	**b.** Main idea:	**c.** Main idea: Lack of a bite or scratch is not a weakness in the theory Poe died of rabies.
2. a. Supporting evidence:	**b.** Supporting evidence:	**c.** Supporting evidence: Over the last 20 years, only 24% of victims could remember contact with a rabid animal.
3. a. Compare and contrast:	**b.** Compare and contrast:	**c.** Compare and contrast:
4. a. Make connections: I met someone whose relative died of a rabies bite. I was surprised to learn that could still happen these days.	**b.** Make connections:	**c.** Make connections:

Synthesis statement: _____

_____

A Country Divided
Lives in the Crossfire

Reading Skill: Synthesizing Sources

When you research a topic, it is a good idea to use different types of sources to get a balanced point of view. Here are some guidelines:

- Decide if your source is a **primary source**—a firsthand, or eyewitness, account—or a **secondary source**—a secondhand account of events in which the writer did not participate.
- Determine the author's **purpose** and **audience.** Why was the source written? Whom was it written for?
- **Compare** and **contrast** the main ideas of the sources. Do they agree or disagree?
- **Evaluate** the authors' arguments. Do they use **facts** or only **opinions**?
- **Connect** your sources to your prior knowledge.
- **Synthesize** the information from your sources to come to **conclusions** about the topic.

Into the Book Excerpts

For hundreds of years, Ireland has been torn apart by a struggle between Catholics and Protestants. This often violent power struggle has become known as the Troubles. The two excerpts you are about to read will give you information from two different sources. "A Country Divided" tells how the conflict began and what is being done to end it. In "Lives in the Crossfire," you'll find out what it is like to grow up on a battleground.

BASED ON THE BOOK EXCERPTS

A Country Divided

By Patricia McMahon

Lives in the Crossfire

By Laurel Holliday

SYNTHESIZING SOURCES

After reading the first ten lines, I'd say the author's purpose is to inform. It sounds a lot like a textbook so far. The text gives lots of historical facts. This would probably be a good source for background information.

VOCABULARY

I'm always being told to be more *tolerant* of my little sister, and I know that means to be more accepting and respectful. So I think *intolerance* in line 12 must mean "disrespect."

SYNTHESIZING SOURCES

Is this a primary source (a firsthand account) or a secondary source (a secondhand account)? How can you tell?

_____

_____

_____

_____

_____

_____

A Country Divided

based on an excerpt from *One Belfast Boy*
by Patricia McMahon

> **YOU NEED TO KNOW** This excerpt has been adapted from an introductory section of *One Belfast Boy*. The introduction includes a brief history of the conflict in Ireland. The remainder of the book tells the story, in words and photographs, of an eleven-year-old boy named Liam Leathem. Liam is a Catholic in Belfast, Northern Ireland, who has never known a Protestant person in his life.

In 1170, King Henry II of England declared himself also king of Ireland. England gradually, and with great bloodshed, took control of Ireland. For hundreds of years, Ireland was ruled—against the wishes of the Irish people—as a colony of the British Empire.

5 Beginning in 1609, England's King James I offered land in Ireland to Scottish settlers if they would move to Ireland and farm. The land was taken away from the Irish.

The Irish called these new arrivals the strangers. They were people with a different language and way of life. Most important,
10 they had a different religion. The Irish were Catholic. The strangers taking over their land were Protestant. At that time a terrible intolerance existed between different faiths.

New English laws said that Catholics could not own land, vote, or work for the government. They could not become lawyers. They
15 were not allowed to speak the Irish language. The English banned the study of Irish history or literature. Forbidden to hold Mass, priests were forced to leave Ireland. In 1800, Great Britain passed the Act of Union. It declared Ireland to be part of the United Kingdom of Great Britain and Ireland.

Adapted from *One Belfast Boy* by Patricia McMahon. Copyright © 1999 by Patricia McMahon. Retold by Holt, Rinehart and Winston. All rights reserved. Reproduced by permission of **Clarion Books/Houghton Mifflin Company.**

20   The Irish fought for their freedom. They fought with words as
well as with weapons. When Catholics regained the vote in 1829,
they tried to influence English Parliament[1] to change the laws.

       In 1916, on Easter Monday, a small rebellion broke out in
Dublin, Ireland's capital. The British army quickly defeated the
25 rebels and shot sixteen of the leaders. Many men and women went
to jail, including some that had not been involved. Anger grew. More
people joined Sinn Fein,[2] a group working for Irish freedom. (In
Gaelic, the Irish language, Sinn Fein means "ourselves alone.")
Some people joined the IRA, the Irish Republican Army. Led by
30 Michael Collins, the outnumbered IRA managed to inflict[3] losses on
the superior British forces.

       But the Irish Protestants believed Ireland should remain part of
the United Kingdom. "No surrender" became their motto. Most of the
Protestants lived in the north, which they called Ulster. Their cry
35 was "Ulster will fight, and Ulster will be right."

       In 1920, the British met with the Irish for peace talks. The
British finally agreed to Irish demands for self-government. But
Ireland, Britain said, must be divided. Most of mainly Protestant
Ulster would become Northern Ireland.

40   In the end, Ireland took the offer. But there was great anger
over the country's division. Civil war broke out. Friends and relatives
turned on one another. In 1921, most of the Irish gained their
freedom. But the Catholics of Northern Ireland remained under
British rule. Catholics there still could not vote unless they owned
45 land, which few did.

       The work of people like Dr. Martin Luther King, Jr., inspired the
Catholics. In 1968, they began a series of protest marches across
Northern Ireland. The government forbade the marches. Mobs
attacked Catholic homes and churches.

50   The Irish Republican Army became active again. The battles
grew worse. One day in 1972 became known as Bloody Sunday.
On that day, British soldiers killed fourteen unarmed protesters.

---

1. **English Parliament:** a branch of government with the power to make laws for the country,
   similar to the United States Congress.
2. **Sinn Fein** (SHIHN FAYN).
3. **inflict:** cause; impose.

Your TURN

VOCABULARY

Circle any words in lines
20–22 that help you
understand what *influence*
means in line 22.

Your TURN

SYNTHESIZING SOURCES

Re-read lines 36–45. Does this
passage contain the author's
thoughts and feelings, or just
facts? Write your answer on
the line below. Then, in the
passage, underline the
evidence for your answer.

Here's HOW

VOCABULARY

I know *forbid* means "not allow."
I'm pretty sure *forbade* (line 48)
is just the past tense of *forbid*,
so it means "not allowed."

Northern Ireland became a battleground. Both sides made bombs and blew up buildings.

55 By 1999, more than 3,200 people had died in the fighting called "The Troubles." They died over the question "Are we British or are we Irish?" There are still two answers to that question. The deaths have not changed this.

People on both sides keep working to stop the fighting. A 60 peace agreement was signed in 1998. A new government of Northern Ireland guarantees the rights of Catholics. But some say there will be no peace until the whole island is one country. Others say there will be no peace if that ever happens.

Lives in the Crossfire

based on excerpts from *Children of "the Troubles"*
by Laurel Holliday

YOU NEED TO KNOW The two introductory paragraphs below were adapted from the diary entries of two Irish children—eighteen-year-old Sharon Ingram and eleven-year-old Bridie Murphy.

December 20, 1976. I would love to sleep some Christmas night with the curtains open. I would like nothing but glass between me and the stars. But [IRA] bombs silence my wishes, for a while at least.

—*Sharon*

5 *April 28, 1994. Living on this street scares me. I am afraid the Protestants across the street will come and kill us. They have shot people in our street eleven times. I don't know why they want to kill us.*

—*Bridie*

Children in Northern Ireland live in a mostly Protestant or mostly
10 Catholic neighborhood. They go to a Catholic or a Protestant school. Their friends are one religion or the other. They shop in their "own" shops. They have their own clubs. When they die, they will go to segregated graveyards.

Even taxicab companies divide along religious lines. Some
15 taxicabs head to Catholic neighborhoods and others to Protestant. In some parts of the country, painted sidewalks signal religious loyalties.

To survive, children learn these differences. They also learn differences in language and point of view. Such differences set
20 them apart from one another all their lives. A city in Northern Ireland

---

From the diary of Sharon Ingram adapted from *Children of "The Troubles": Our Lives in the Crossfire of Northern Ireland* by Laurel Holliday. Copyright © 1997 by Sharon Ingram. Retold by Holt, Rinehart and Winston. Published by Pocket Books, a division of Simon & Schuster, New York, 1997. Reproduced by permission of **Sharon Ingram.**

From Editor's Introduction adapted from *Children of "The Troubles,"* edited by Laurel Holliday. Copyright © 1997 by Laurel Holliday. Retold by Holt, Rinehart and Winston. Reproduced by permission of **Atria Books, an imprint of Simon & Schuster Adult Publishing Group.**

SYNTHESIZING SOURCES

This selection begins with two diary excerpts, which are primary sources. I don't think it's going to be as factual as the first selection. These excerpts tell about the children's fears and wishes.

VOCABULARY

I know what segregation is. It's keeping things, like races of people, separate. So *segregated* in line 13 must mean "separate."

SYNTHESIZING SOURCES

Is the text after the diary excerpts a primary or secondary source?

_____

_____

SYNTHESIZING SOURCES

This selection is less formal than the first one. The speaker addresses the reader directly in lines 24–27. The first selection had more of a textbook style.

SYNTHESIZING SOURCES

By now, you should recognize that this source has a different focus than "A Country Divided." Re-read lines 24–37. Identify the author's purpose and audience, and write your answers on the lines below.

• Purpose: _____

_____

_____

_____

_____

_____

_____

_____

_____

_____

• Audience: _____

_____

_____

_____

_____

_____

_____

is called Derry by Catholics and Londonderry by Protestants. Catholics call the Troubles a war. Protestants call the Troubles a terrorist uprising.

25   Suppose you're a Catholic child. Your family wants Ireland to be one country. You say you live in the North of Ireland. You might also call your homeland the Six Counties. Now suppose you're a Protestant child. You call your homeland Northern Ireland or Ulster.

    From birth, these children are set on different paths. But starting at age seven, some Catholic and Protestant children become more 30 involved in the adult world. Adults from both sides force children to run dangerous errands and even put together and hide weapons.

    Most people of Northern Ireland hate the fighting. Many take no part in it themselves, but just about every family has had members beaten, tortured, or killed. The children have witnessed it 35 all. This is not a war where adults go away to fight the enemy. It's an everyday, in-your-face war. The enemy lives on the next block. The enemy speaks (almost) the same language.

Synthesizing Sources

Source Chart

When you begin to research a subject, it is helpful to keep track of the kinds of sources you gather. One good way to do that is to keep a **source chart.** Recording information about your sources in the chart will help you **synthesize** the information into one big picture.

The two selections you just read are about the long-standing political conflict in Ireland. However, they contain different types of information. Use the chart below to compare "A Country Divided" with "Lives in the Crossfire." Some items are filled in for you.

Features	"A Country Divided"	"Lives in the Crossfire"
1. a. Author's Purpose:	**b.** To inform. To give historical background.	**c.**
2. a. Intended Audience:	**b.**	**c.**
3. a. Type of Information: • Objective facts? • Historical background? • Author's thoughts and feelings? • A combination?	**b.** Mostly facts and historical background. Very little of author's thoughts and feelings.	**c.**

The Gift of the Magi

Literary Focus: Situational Irony

What would you think of a movie that was completely predictable?
You'd probably think it was pretty boring. Stories by good writers
are often very *un*predictable. When something happens that is the
opposite of what you expected, it is called **situational irony.**
Situational irony remind us that many things in life turn out
differently from what we expect.

Reading Skill: Making Predictions

You may have heard someone describe an exciting book as "a
real page turner." When you keep wondering what will happen next,
you've got a page turner in your hands. Try to predict what will
happen as you read "The Gift of the Magi," and see how often the
writer surprises you. You may want to keep track of your **predictions**
in a chart like this one:

Situation	My Prediction	What Really Happens

Into the Story

O. Henry's real name was William Sydney Porter. He worked as a
bank teller in Austin, Texas, until he was accused of stealing
$1,000 from the bank. Porter was arrested, tried, and sentenced
to five years in prison. No one knows whether he really stole the
money. Porter served three years of his sentence, and he wrote more
than a dozen stories while in prison. He left prison in 1901 and
moved to New York. He wrote about New York City and the people
who lived there until his death in 1910.

O. Henry

The Gift of the Magi

MAKING PREDICTIONS

Why is Della saving money? In line 7, I get a clue about what is going on. I think Della has been saving money to buy someone a Christmas gift.

Your
TURN

MAKING PREDICTIONS

In lines 28–33, Della is thinking about something. What do you think she is considering? Write your answer on the lines below. Then, underline any clues you see in the passage.

_____

_____

_____

_____

_____

_____

Della had saved one dollar and eighty-seven cents. That was all. And sixty cents of it was in pennies. She had saved the pennies one and two at a time by bargaining with the grocer, the vegetable seller, and the butcher to lower their prices. At times, her cheeks

5 had burned with shame, for she was certain these sellers thought she was stingy. She counted her money three times. One dollar and eighty-seven cents. And the next day was Christmas.

Della decided there was nothing she could do except flop down on the shabby little couch and cry. So she did.

10 Della and her husband lived in a furnished apartment costing $8 per week. It didn't exactly look like the home of a beggar, but it had no extras, either.

In the entrance hall below, there was a letterbox that a letter couldn't fit in and a doorbell that didn't ring. There was also a card

15 with the name *"Mr. James Dillingham Young"* on it.

For a short time, Mr. James Dillingham Young had done well for himself, making $30 per week.[1] Now, his pay had shrunk to $20. With his pay cut, he'd lost his sense of place in the outside world. But whenever he came home, he was joyously greeted and hugged

20 by his wife, Della. Which was all very good.

Della finished her crying and dried her cheeks. She stood by the window and looked out dully at a gray cat walking a gray fence in a gray backyard. Tomorrow would be Christmas Day, and after all her saving, she had only $1.87 to buy Jim a present. There were

25 always more expenses than she thought. She had spent many happy hours planning a gift for him, something fine and rare and perfect, something worthy of her special Jim.

Suddenly Della turned from the window and looked at herself in the tall, old mirror. Her eyes were shining brightly, but her face

30 had lost its color within twenty seconds. Quickly she pulled down her hair and let it fall loosely around her.

Jim and Della were proud of two things, Jim's gold watch, which had been his father's and his grandfather's, and Della's hair. Della's beautiful, shiny hair now fell below her knees. A few of her

35 tears splashed on the worn carpet.

_____

1. **$30 per week:** equal to about $600 today.

But she put on her coat and hat and, with a brilliant sparkle still in her eyes, hurried out. She stopped at a shop with a sign that read "Madame Sofronie. Hair Goods of All Kinds." Della ran up the flight of stairs. Panting, she collected herself and said to Madame
40 Sofronie, "Will you buy my hair?"

"Let's have a look at it," said Madame.

Della let down her beautiful hair.

Madame lifted the mass of hair. "Twenty dollars," she said.

"Give it to me quickly," said Della.

45 For two hours, Della searched for Jim's present. At last she found a platinum fob chain,[2] worthy of The Watch. It was like Jim —quiet and valuable.

She paid twenty-one dollars. With that chain, instead of the old leather strap he used now, Jim could proudly check the time in
50 public.

At home, Della worked with her curling iron. After forty minutes, her head was covered with tiny curls. She studied herself in the mirror. "If Jim doesn't kill me right away," she said to herself, "he'll say I look like a chorus girl. But what could I do with a dollar and
55 eighty-seven cents!"

When she heard him on the stairs, her face turned white for a minute. She whispered, "Please, God, make him think I am still pretty."

The door opened and Jim entered. His eyes fixed on Della. He
60 did not show anger, surprise, disapproval, or horror. He had an expression she could not read.

Della went to hug him.

"Jim, darling," she cried, "don't look at me that way. I sold my hair because I couldn't have lived without giving you a Christmas
65 present. It'll grow. You won't mind, will you?"

"You've cut your hair?" asked Jim.

"Cut it off and sold it. Don't you like me just as well, anyhow? I'm me without my hair."

"You say your hair is gone?" he said. He seemed stunned.

70 "It's sold. It's Christmas Eve. Be good to me, because I sold it for you. I love you dearly."

---

2. fob chain: short chain meant to be attached to a pocket watch.

Here's HOW

MAKING PREDICTIONS

I had a feeling Della was going to do something extreme to get money for a gift. Lines 36–40 still surprised me, though. I didn't think Della would sell one of the things she and Jim were most proud of.

Your TURN

VOCABULARY

The word *collected* (line 39) can mean "gathered together" or "regained control of." What meaning does it have here?

_____

_____

Your TURN

MAKING PREDICTIONS

Re-read lines 59–69. Is Jim's reaction what you expected? Why do you think Jim seems stunned but not upset when he sees Della's hair?

_____

_____

_____

_____

_____

_____

Jim came out of his trance and hugged Della.

"Don't mind me, Dell," he said. "You could cut or shave your hair any way you like and I wouldn't love you less. But if you unwrap
75 that package, you may see why I was so surprised."

Della tore at the paper and string. She screamed for joy and then began crying. Jim rose to comfort her.

He had given her The Combs—the set of combs, side and back, that Della had wanted for a long, long time. They would have
80 been perfect in her long hair. She had longed for them without ever believing she'd own them. And now they were hers, but the beautiful hair to wear them in was gone.

She smiled at Jim. "My hair grows fast!"

And then Della cried, "Oh, oh!"
85 Jim hadn't seen his beautiful present yet. She held it out to him eagerly.

"Isn't it a dandy, Jim? You'll have to look at the time one hundred times a day now. Give me your watch. I want to see how the fob looks on it."
90 Jim didn't hand over the watch. "Dell," he said, "let's put away our Christmas presents. They're too nice to use right now. I sold the watch to get the money to buy your combs."

The Magi,[3] as you know, were wise men. They brought gifts to the baby Jesus. They were the first people to give Christmas
95 presents. They were wise, and probably so were their gifts. Here you have read the story of two foolish children in an apartment. They unwisely gave up the greatest treasures of their house for each other. But of all who give and receive gifts, those like these two are wisest. Everywhere they are the wisest. They are the Magi.

---

3. **Magi** (MAY jy).

Situational Irony

In **situational irony,** events turn out to be the opposite of what you expected. Authors use irony in fiction to surprise the reader. Also, in real life it is impossible to predict the future exactly. Things often turn out differently from what you had hoped or expected.

Explore O. Henry's use of situational irony in "The Gift of the Magi" by filling in the following chart. The first item has been done for you.

Expectation	Reality
1. Della has saved her money expecting to buy Jim a wonderful Christmas present.	She has saved only a fraction of what she needs, so she sells her hair on Christmas Eve to get the money.
2. Della thinks the watch chain will be the perfect gift for Jim.	
3. Jim thinks Della will be happy with the combs she has admired for so long.	

The Lady, or the Tiger?

Literary Focus: Ambiguity

You notice your friend talking to someone you thought she hated. What does it mean? Have they become friends? Is there another reason for the conversation? Without more information the situation is ambiguous. **Ambiguity** occurs when something can be interpreted in different ways. Ambiguity made "The Lady, or the Tiger?" an instant hit. When you finish reading, try to answer the question in the title.

Reading Skills: Making Inferences About Motivation

When you make an **inference** about a character's **motivation,** you make an educated guess about the character's reasons for behaving in a certain way. You base your guess on clues in the text (what the narrator says about the character and what the character says or does) and your own experience. As you read "The Lady, or the Tiger?" think about the motivation of the three characters, especially the king's daughter.

Into the Story

During the Middle Ages an accused person was often given a trial involving a dangerous activity. If the person was not hurt, it was thought that the accused was saved from harm by God and was therefore innocent. Those who were injured or killed were considered guilty. In "The Lady, or the Tiger?" justice is decided in a similar way.

The Lady, or the Tiger?

BASED ON THE STORY BY

Frank R. Stockton

In the very olden time, there lived a half-civilized king. His ideas were sometimes polished and sensible, but often wild and strange. This king had the habit of talking to himself, and when he and himself agreed on a thing, the thing was done. When everything was
5 going smoothly, he was calm and friendly. When there was even a little hitch, he was even calmer and friendlier. For he loved to make the crooked straight and to crush down uneven places.

The king loved his public arena, and there he held exhibitions of manly and beastly courage.
10 He built this arena not just to give the people the opportunity to view dying gladiators or battles between the king's religious enemies and hungry lions. The king had another purpose for the arena. With its mysterious vaults and unseen passages, the arena was a place where crime was punished and virtue was rewarded by the decrees
15 of chance.

When a subject was accused of a crime important enough to interest the king, notice was given that the fate of the accused would be decided in the king's arena. Although this arena was like other arenas in form, its purpose came from the strange fancy of the king
20 himself. Nothing was more important to the king than his own ideas.

When the people gathered in the arena, the king would give a signal, a door would open beneath him, and the accused would come out. Opposite the accused were two doors, side by side and exactly alike. The accused would walk across the arena and open one of the
25 doors. Only chance determined which one he would open. If the accused opened one door, a hungry tiger would come out and tear him apart as punishment for his guilt. The mourners would wail and sad bells would clang. The audience would go slowly homeward, mourning greatly that one so young and fair had died or that one so
30 old and respected had earned so harsh a fate.

But if the accused opened the other door, a lady came out. She would be suitable to his years and station, and they would be immediately married to reward his innocence. It did not matter if the accused was already married with a family, or if he was in love with
35 another woman. The king allowed no interference with his will. A priest would appear, along with joyous singers, and the wedding

would take place immediately, within the arena. Brass bells would ring their merry peals, the people would shout hurrahs, and children would throw flowers in the path of the happy couple.

40 This was the king's way of administering justice. Its perfect fairness was obvious. The criminal could not know which door to open. On some occasions the tiger came out one door. Sometimes it came out the other. The accused was instantly punished or rewarded on the spot. There was no escape from the judgment of the king's
45 arena.

The institution was very popular because people never knew if they were going to see a bloody punishment or a happy wedding. The people were entertained and pleased by the suspense. Even the thinking part of the community thought it was fair. Did not the
50 accused have the matter in his own hands?

The king had a daughter blooming with beauty. She had a soul as passionate and headstrong as the king's. She fell in love with a handsome young man who was brave and fine. But he was from a low social class. He was handsome and brave, and the king's
55 daughter loved him passionately. The love affair moved along happily for many months until the king found out about it. He cast the youth into prison, and the day was chosen for his trial in the king's arena. This was to be a very important trial, and everyone looked forward to it. Never before had a commoner dared to love the daughter of a king.

60 The tiger cages of the kingdom were searched, and the fiercest beast was chosen. The ranks of maidens were likewise searched. The king wanted to find the fairest bride. Of course, everyone knew the young man was guilty. He had indeed loved the king's daughter. No one denied this fact, but the workings of the court must go forward.
65 No matter how the affair turned out, the king would take pleasure in it. Events would determine whether the young man had done wrong in loving the king's daughter.

The day arrived. From far and near, crowds came to fill the arena, and more people, unable to get in, waited outside. The king and his
70 court sat in their chairs opposite the two fateful doors— so terrible in their similarity.

Your TURN

MAKING INFERENCES ABOUT MOTIVATION

Based on what you have learned about the king, tell why you think he created this system of justice.

_____

_____

_____

_____

_____

_____

Your TURN

MAKING INFERENCES ABOUT MOTIVATION

In lines 52–53, underline the reasons why the king's daughter loves the young man. Then, circle in line 59 the reason why the king sends him to prison.

Your TURN

MAKING INFERENCES ABOUT MOTIVATION

Why do you think the king has this trial when everyone knows and admits the young man is guilty of loving his daughter? Write your answer on the lines below.

_____

_____

_____

_____

THE LADY, OR THE TIGER?   **73**

MAKING INFERENCES ABOUT MOTIVATION

Many people would not want to be in a place where their lover might be killed by a tiger. Why do you think the princess comes to the arena for the trial?

_____

_____

_____

Your **TURN**

MAKING INFERENCES ABOUT MOTIVATION

The prince goes straight to the door the princess signals. Why doesn't he hesitate in following her signal?

_____

_____

_____

_____

_____

_____

Your **TURN**

AMBIGUITY

The author does not tell whether the lady or the tiger comes out of the door, so the ending is ambiguous. How do you think the story ended?

_____

_____

All was ready, and a signal was given. The lover of the princess walked into the arena. He was tall and fair, and a low hum of admiration and anxiety rose from the crowd. No wonder the princess 75 loved him! What a terrible thing for him to be there!

The youth entered the arena, and bowed to the king. He also bowed to the princess. Her passionate soul would not allow her to miss this occasion, for she had thought of nothing else. Her lover would be killed—or he would marry another.

80 The princess had done what no one else had ever accomplished. She had found out the secret of the doors. She knew behind which door was the tiger and behind which door was the lovely maiden. The doors were thick. The young man could hear no sound coming through them. Only the princess knew the secret.

85 Not only did the princess know behind which door was the maiden, she also knew who this maiden was. She was one of the fairest women of the court, and she was someone the princess hated. She had seen, or imagined she had seen, the woman looking admiringly at her lover. She had seen them talking together, and the 90 princess hated this young woman with all the passion of her nature.

Her lover turned to look up at her. Because their souls and minds had long been one, the young man instantly knew that the princess had found out the secret of the doors, and that she knew which door held the tiger and which the lovely maiden. He understood her nature 95 very well and had expected her to find out the secret.

He glanced at her as if to ask "Which?" The princess indicated her decision with a wave of her right hand. Only her lover saw this gesture. The eyes of the audience were fixed on the arena. The young man turned, and with a firm and quick step, he walked across the 100 empty space. Without any hesitation, he went to the door on the right and opened it.

The question of the princess' decision is not to be lightly considered. It is not for me to presume to be the one person able to answer it, and so I leave it with all of you: Which came out of the 105 opened door—the lady or the tiger?

Ambiguity Chart

An ambiguous situation can be interpreted in more than one way. To explore the **ambiguity** in "The Lady, or the Tiger?" fill in details from the text that support each interpretation. One detail has been filled in for you. Then, decide which version you prefer. Remember, there is no correct answer. Either could be true.

Which comes out of the door?

The Lady	The Tiger
	The princess hates and is jealous of the lady.

My decision: _____

_____

A Defense of the Jury System

Reading Skill: Evaluating an Argument

An argument is not just a disagreement. In its more formal meaning an **argument** is a series of statements made to convince you of something. When you **evaluate an argument,** you analyze it to decide whether it is believable. Here are some tips for evaluating an argument:

- **Understand the claim**, or point, the author is trying to make.
- **Identify the support** the author uses to back up the claim. Support comes in several forms:
  - **Logical appeals.** These are the **reasons** for the claim.
  - **Evidence.** Facts, statistics (number facts), examples, and quotations or opinions from experts are types of evidence.
  - **Analogies.** These comparisons of something complex to something more familiar help you understand the claim.
  - **Emotional appeals.** An author may appeal to your emotions, instead of to your reason, by using **loaded words** (words that connect to feelings) or by telling anecdotes (brief stories).
- **Identify the intent.** Ask yourself why the author is making the argument.

Into the Essay

"The Lady, or the Tiger?" describes a system of justice in which innocence or guilt are decided entirely by chance. Does that system seem fair to you? How fair is our justice system in the United States? Read the following persuasive essay to learn what one expert thinks.

A Defense of the Jury System

BASED ON THE ARTICLE BY

Thomas M. Ross, Esq.

Here's
HOW

EVALUATING AN ARGUMENT

The title of the essay is "A Defense of the Jury System." But in the first two paragraphs, the author only says what's wrong with juries. I think he is first stating the opposite point of view so that he can then argue against it.

Your
TURN

EVALUATING AN ARGUMENT

In lines 14–18, underline the opinions of experts that the author uses as evidence to support his argument.

Your
TURN

EVALUATING AN ARGUMENT

Underline the reasons, or logical appeals, the author uses in lines 19–28.

Your
TURN

EVALUATING AN ARGUMENT

In your own words, state the main claim, or point the author is making, in this essay.

_____

_____

_____

_____

The jury system is often attacked for delivering verdicts that sometimes seem irrational. Some cases are well known. For example, one fast-food company was forced to pay $2.7 million to a woman who had spilled hot coffee on her lap.

5　Juries are criticized for deciding cases based on prejudice and emotion rather than relying on the evidence and the law. It is also said that they are unable to understand the complex issues.

These critics are like those who say that voters are irrational, ill-informed, and easily influenced by simple slogans. But no one favors 10　doing away with the vote. Democracy, it is said, "is the worst form of government—except for all the others." The same can be said of the jury system: It is the worst system of justice—except for all the others.

Much of the criticism of the jury system is unfair, because most jurors try to do a good job. According to one survey, most jurors said 15　they would rather be tried by their peers than by a panel of judges. Nearly all of the judges in a Texas survey thought that jurors do at least "moderately well." In fact, more than half of those judges said they would rather have their case decided by a jury instead of a judge.

Some people believe that having judges decide all cases would 20　improve the system, but judges, like jurors, are human beings who can make mistakes. Also, judges do not represent society, since most of them are still male, Caucasian, and from middle-class and well-to-do backgrounds. Women, minorities, and less wealthy people continue to be underrepresented in the court system.

25　On the other hand, jurors come from a widely varied group of people. They are required to be fair and impartial. A jury reflects different backgrounds and points of view. The system helps make sure that a verdict will not be based on one person's opinions.

Human beings are not perfect—we make mistakes. The jury 30　system is not perfect, either. Despite its flaws, however, it is the best means we have to ensure justice in a democracy, for it guarantees that the point of view of all citizens will be represented.

Evaluating an Argument

When you **evaluate an argument,** you analyze it to decide if it is believable. You look at how the author **supports** his or her claims. Practice evaluating an argument by matching the statements from "A Defense of the Jury System" in the column on the left with the types of support listed in the column on the right. One has been done for you. (If you don't remember what the terms mean, look back at the definitions on page 76.)

Quotes from the Essay	Types of Support
_____ **1.** Human beings are not perfect—we make mistakes.	**a.** analogy
	b. fact
	c. expert opinion
___b___ **2.** Women, minorities, and less wealthy people continue to be underrepresented in the court system.	**d.** loaded words
	e. statistic
_____ **3.** Democracy, it is said, "is the worst form of government—except for all the others." The same can be said of the jury system.	
_____ **4.** Nearly all of the judges in a Texas survey thought that jurors do at least "moderately well."	
_____ **5.** In fact, more than half of those judges said they would rather have their case decided by a jury instead of a judge.	

Letter to President Roosevelt, 1939

Reading Skill: Paraphrasing and Connecting

When you read informational materials, it is important to decide
what *you* think about what the writer is saying. Two useful steps in
making your decisions are paraphrasing and connecting.

- **Paraphrasing.** You paraphrase to be sure you understand what
  the author is saying. In paraphrasing, you restate the text in
  your own words. You restate all the ideas in the order in which
  they appear.

- **Connecting.** When you connect, you relate the ideas in the text to
  what you already know about the topic or the writer. If you
  already know a lot about a topic, for instance, you will be able to
  judge whether the information you are reading is accurate. Even
  a little prior knowledge can help you understand the ideas better.

I learned in my social studies class about the time we dropped an atomic bomb on Japan. It caused huge damaged.

Into the Letter

In August of 1939, the famous physicist Albert Einstein wrote
a letter warning President Franklin D. Roosevelt that powerful
bombs could be developed from nuclear energy. Six years later, on
August 6, 1945, the first atomic bomb to be used in war was
dropped on Hiroshima, Japan, leading to the end of World War II.
The bomb destroyed almost five square miles of the city and killed
many thousands of people. Many others died later from illnesses
caused by radiation from the bomb.

Letter to President Roosevelt, 1939

BASED ON THE LETTER BY
Albert Einstein

Sir:

Some recent scientific work leads me to believe that uranium may become a new and important source of energy in the immediate future. Your administration needs to pay attention, and, if necessary,

5 act quickly. I believe, therefore, that it is my duty to call your attention to the following facts and recommendations:

In the last four months it has become more likely that, very soon, a nuclear chain reaction could be set up in a large mass of uranium. Huge amounts of power and large quantities of new radium-like

10 elements would be created. This new possibility might also lead to the building of a new type of extremely powerful bombs. A single bomb of this type, delivered by boat and exploded in a port, could destroy the entire port and some of the surrounding area. Such bombs might be too heavy to be transported by air, however.

15 The United States does not have much high-quality uranium. There is some good ore in Canada and Czechoslovakia. The most important source of uranium is the Belgian Congo.

You may want to start contact between the Administration and the physicists working on this project. If you give the task to someone

20 you trust, he could keep different government departments informed. He could also recommend ways that the United States could get more uranium. He could raise private funds to speed up experimental work. He could also seek the help from industrial labs, which have the necessary equipment.

25 I understand Germany has stopped the sale of uranium from the Czechoslovakian mines. This may be because the German Under-Secretary of State is involved in uranium research taking place in Berlin.

Yours very truly,
Albert Einstein

Paraphrasing and Connecting

Two strategies for understanding what you read are paraphrasing and connecting. When you **paraphrase,** you restate all the ideas in your own words. When you **connect,** you relate the ideas to what you already know. In the first box below, restate the ideas in the letter. (The first paragraph is paraphrased on page 82, so start with the second.) In the second box, write down what you already know about the topic. In the third box, respond by saying what you think of or about the letter.

Paraphrase:

Connect:

Respond:

The Seven Ages of Man

Literary Focus: Extended Metaphor

If your teacher says your classroom is a zoo, do you know what he or she means? Your teacher is using a **metaphor** to describe your class's behavior. A metaphor is a figure of speech that compares one thing to another. So when your teacher says your classroom is a zoo, he or she means it's *like* a zoo because the students are acting like wild animals. A metaphor that is developed, or *extends,* over several lines of a poem is called an **extended metaphor.**

Reading Skill: Paraphrasing a Poem

Figures of speech make poems more fun to read. However, they aren't always the clearest way of saying something. A poem that uses figures of speech to present complex ideas and comparisons can be hard to understand. You can understand a poem better if you **paraphrase** it. To paraphrase simply means to rewrite it in your own words. Take a look at this sample paraphrase from "The Seven Ages of Man."

Original	Paraphrase
"All the world's a stage, / And all the men and women merely players;"	The world is like a stage. People are like actors in a play.

Into the Poem

Shakespeare's plays often pause for a brilliant speech by one of the characters. Among the most famous speeches are the St. Crispin's Day speech from *Henry V,* Marc Antony's funeral speech from *Julius Caesar,* and "The Seven Ages of Man" from *As You Like It.* It makes sense that the most famous English playwright would compare the ages of human life to a seven-act play.

William Shakespeare

THE SEVEN AGES OF MAN

Here's HOW

EXTENDED METAPHOR

I can see the simple metaphor in line 1. The world is compared to a stage, like in a theater. As I read on, I can see that this metaphor extends throughout the speech. Each act of the play represents a period, or "age," of a person's life.

Your TURN

PARAPHRASING A POEM

Re-read the "Last scene of all" in lines 25–28. On the lines below, rewrite this sentence in your own words. You may have to use more words than Shakespeare did to get the meaning across in modern English.

_____

_____

_____

_____

_____

_____

_____

_____

_____

_____

_____

_____

_____

_____

All the world's a stage,

And all the men and women merely players;

They have their exits and their entrances,

And one man in his time plays many parts,

5   His acts being seven ages. At first the infant,

Mewling and puking in the nurse's arms;

And then the whining schoolboy, with his satchel

And shining morning face, creeping like snail

Unwillingly to school. And then the lover,

10   Sighing like furnace, with a woeful ballad

Made to his mistress' eyebrow. Then a soldier,

Full of strange oaths, and bearded like the pard,[1]

Jealous in honor, sudden and quick in quarrel,

Seeking the bubble reputation

15   Even in the cannon's mouth. And then the justice,[2]

In fair round belly with good capon[3] lined,

With eyes severe and beard of formal cut,

Full of wise saws[4] and modern instances;

And so he plays his part. The sixth age shifts

20   Into the lean and slippered pantaloon,[5]

With spectacles on nose and pouch on side;

His youthful hose,[6] well saved, a world too wide

For his shrunk shank; and his big manly voice,

Turning again toward childish treble, pipes

25   And whistles in his sound. Last scene of all,

That ends this strange eventful history,

Is second childishness and mere oblivion,

Sans[7] teeth, sans eyes, sans taste, sans everything.

1. **pard:** leopard.
2. **justice:** judge.
3. **capon:** fat chicken.
4. **saws:** sayings.
5. **pantaloon:** silly old man.
6. **hose:** stockings.
7. **sans:** without.

IN OTHER WORDS The world is like a stage, and people are like actors. People play different roles throughout their lives. The play of life is divided into seven acts. For each act a person takes on a different role.

The first role he plays is a baby, crying and throwing up all over his caregiver.

The next role is a student, carrying a school bag, walking very slowly to school because he doesn't want to get there.

Next, he plays a lover, filled with the aches of young love. He gives great, dramatic sighs as he sings sad songs dedicated to his sweetheart's eyebrow.

Then, he is a foul-mouthed soldier with a beard like a wild animal's. He is always defending his honor and fighting to make his reputation, even at the risk of his life.

Next, he plays the role of an adult with a respectable job, like a judge. He has a fat belly from eating good food. He looks harsh, and his beard is neatly cut. He is full of wise old sayings and modern stories that prove those sayings are correct.

The sixth role is a silly old man, wearing slippers and reading glasses, and carrying a bag at his side. The clothes he wore when he was young are too big for him now. His voice no longer sounds deep and manly, but instead it is high-pitched, like a child's.

The last role ends the strange play that has been his life. His body and mind are failing him, and he's like a newborn baby again. He's lost his teeth, his senses, and everything else.

Extended Metaphor

An **extended metaphor** is a comparison that is developed, or extended, over several lines of a poem. In "The Seven Ages of Man," Shakespeare compares life to a play in seven acts.

Fill out the chart below to apply this famous metaphor to your life. In the first column, write the age you would be during each act of the play. In the second column, write the roles *you* might play during each act. A sample answer is provided for Act One.

My Life in Seven Acts		
Act	**Your Ages**	**Your Roles**
One (lines 5–6)	1-4 years old	infant, baby, toddler, day-care or nursery-school student
Two (lines 7–9)		
Three (lines 9–11)		
Four (lines 11–15)		
Five (lines 15–19)		
Six (lines 19–25)		
Seven (lines 25–28)		

Paraphrasing

When you **paraphrase,** you restate all the ideas in a text in your own words. Paraphrasing helps you understand what you are reading. To paraphrase lines in a poem, you may have to explain what the figures of speech mean. This may make your paraphrase longer than the original lines.

To help you understand Shakespeare's famous lines, paraphrase the quotes in the chart below. If you have trouble understanding the lines, check the summary on page 87. Then, re-read the lines, and restate them in your own words.

Quotation	My Paraphrase
1. All the world's a stage, / And all the men and women merely players; / They have their exits and their entrances, / And one man in his time plays many parts, / His acts being seven ages.	
2. And then the whining schoolboy, with his satchel / And shining morning face, creeping like snail / Unwillingly to school.	
3. Then a soldier, / Full of strange oaths, and bearded like the pard, / Jealous in honor, sudden and quick in quarrel, / Seeking the bubble reputation / Even in the cannon's mouth.	

I Wandered Lonely as a Cloud

Literary Skills: Rhythm and Meter

The musical quality in poems comes from repetition, or **rhythm.**
Some poets create rhythm by arranging the words so that the lines
repeat a regular pattern of stressed and unstressed syllables. This
kind of regular pattern is called **meter.** When you **scan** a poem, you
mark the stressed syllables with the symbol ´ and the unstressed
syllables with the symbol ˘. This is how you would scan the first line
of William Wordsworth's famous poem:

Ĭ wánderĕd lónelў ás ă clo̍ud

Reading Skill: Reading a Poem

When you are trying to find the meter in a poem, you put extra stress
on the stressed syllables. But that is not how you read a poem when
you want to get the meaning across. Here are some tips for reading
poems for their meaning:

- Forget about the meter. (It will still be there, kind of like the
  backbone of the poem.)
- Most poems are written in sentences. Look for punctuation
  telling you where the sentences begin and end.
- If lines are hard to understand, look for the subject, verb, and
  object. Decide what words the phrases and clauses modify.
- Do not stop at the end of a line if there is no period, question
  mark, or exclamation point. Pause only briefly for commas,
  semicolons, and dashes.
- Read the poem aloud. The sound of a poem contributes to its
  meaning.

Into the Poem

This poem captures very precisely a special moment that happened
over two hundred years ago—on April 15, 1802. We know the exact
date because another person was there at the time. The poet's sister,
Dorothy, captured the very same scene in her journal.

I Wandered Lonely as a Cloud

William Wordsworth

I wandered lonely as a cloud
That floats on high o'er vales and hills,
When all at once I saw a crowd,
A host, of golden daffodils,
5 Beside the lake, beneath the trees,
Fluttering and dancing in the breeze.

IN OTHER WORDS I was out walking one day, feeling lonely—like a cloud floating high above the valleys and hills. Suddenly, next to a lake and under some trees, I saw a field of yellow daffodils. As they fluttered in the breeze, they seemed to me to be like a crowd of people dancing.

Continuous as the stars that shine
And twinkle on the Milky Way,
They stretched in never-ending line
10 Along the margin of a bay;
Ten thousand saw I at a glance,
Tossing their heads in sprightly dance.

IN OTHER WORDS The flowers seemed to be endless, like the stars that twinkle in the Milky Way galaxy. They stretched endlessly along the shore of the lake. I could see ten thousand with just a short look.

The waves beside them danced, but they
Outdid the sparkling waves in glee;
15 A poet could not but be gay,
In such a jocund° company;
I gazed—and gazed—but little thought
What wealth the show to me had brought.

° **jocund** (JAHK uhnd): merry.

IN OTHER WORDS The waves from the lake also seemed like they were dancing, but as sparkling and beautiful as the waves were, the daffodils outdid them. I couldn't help but be happy, amid such a happy group. I watched them for a long time, but I didn't really think of how much the sight of these daffodils would mean to me someday.

For oft, when on my couch I lie
20 In vacant or in pensive mood,
They flash upon that inward eye
Which is the bliss of solitude;
And then my heart with pleasure fills,
And dances with the daffodils.

IN OTHER WORDS Now, when I am lying on my couch, thinking mindlessly or even thinking deep, sad thoughts, the vision of those daffodils appears to me. I see them in my mind's eye, which is one of the joys of being alone. Then, my heart fills with pleasure, and it feels as if it is with the daffodils, dancing beside the lake.

READING A POEM

Read the third stanza (lines 13–18, on page 92) aloud. Notice how the sound of the poem adds to the idea of the happiness produced by the gaily bobbing daffodils.

RHYTHM AND METER

Use the scanning symbols you learned on page 90 to mark the stressed and unstressed syllables of the last line of the poem. Put your marks on the poem, right above the line. Is the meter the same as that shown on page 90 for the first line of the poem?

_____

_____

Reading a Poem

On the copy of "I Wandered Lonely as a Cloud" below, put a slash next to each period, semicolon, or comma that ends a full thought. Circle the subject and underline the verb in each of these thoughts. (The first stanza has been done for you.) Next, read the poem aloud two or three times. Finally, write down an adjective or two that describes how the poem makes you feel.

(I) wandered lonely as a cloud
That floats on high o'er vales and hills, /
When all at once (I) saw a crowd,
A host, of golden daffodils,
5   Beside the lake, beneath the trees,
Fluttering and dancing in the breeze. /

Continuous as the stars that shine
And twinkle on the Milky Way,
They stretched in never-ending line
10   Along the margin of a bay;
Ten thousand saw I at a glance,
Tossing their heads in sprightly dance.

The waves beside them danced, but they
Outdid the sparkling waves in glee;
15   A poet could not but be gay,
In such a jocund company;
I gazed—and gazed—but little thought
What wealth the show to me had brought.

For oft, when on my couch I lie
20   In vacant or in pensive mood,
They flash upon that inward eye
Which is the bliss of solitude;
And then my heart with pleasure fills,
And dances with the daffodils.

The poem makes me feel _____.

Vocabulary Development

Developing Vocabulary

For each item below, fill in the blank with the correct word from the Word Bank. On the lines following each item, write an original sentence using the word. One item is completed for you.

Word Bank
host
jocund
pensive
solitude

1. Janice had a thoughtful look on her face after the big test.

   She must have been in a _____ mood.

   My sentence: _____

   _____

   _____

2. A _____host_____ of students gathered around the author to get his autograph. There were so many students that we couldn't even see the famous writer in the crowd.

   My sentence: I thought of a host of reasons to stay home from the party. ____

   _____

   _____

3. After striking out four straight times, Sammy stomped to the locker room to get away from his disappointed teammates. I guess he just needed

   some _____.

   My sentence: _____

   _____

   _____

4. The audience laughed and laughed at the crazy antics of the _____ clown. They thought he was really funny.

   My sentence: _____

   _____

   _____

Rising Tides

Reading Skill: Evaluating Arguments

Whenever you read newspaper editorials or other persuasive essays, you have to **evaluate the arguments** to decide if they are believable. To evaluate arguments, follow these steps:

1. **Understand the arguments.** Begin by making sure you understand the writer's claims, opinions, or points. It helps to **paraphrase** the arguments using your own words.

2. **Identify the support.** First, look for the **logical appeals**—the **reasons** the writer gives for his or her opinions—and the **evidence** given to back up each reason. Evidence may consist of these items:
   - **facts** (statements that can be proved)
   - **statistics** (numerical facts)
   - **opinions from experts**

   Then, find **emotional appeals,** such as **loaded words** (words with emotional connections) and **anecdotes** (colorful or personal stories). As you read "Rising Tides," notice the kinds of arguments that Bob Herbert uses in this persuasive essay.

Into the Essay

Most scientists agree that we have changed the earth's atmosphere by releasing huge amounts of carbon dioxide and other gases from our factories and cars. These gases trap heat in our atmosphere and raise the temperature—creating global warming. Some people, though, don't think the warming will be a permanent change or a big problem. Bob Herbert thinks it is a huge problem that we must do something about right now. Read the essay, and decide whether you think he makes his case.

Rising Tides

BASED ON THE OP-ED ARTICLE IN *THE NEW YORK TIMES*, FEBRUARY 22, 2001, BY

Bob Herbert

The easiest approach for now is to pretend it's not happening. It's easier than admitting that the great ice cap on Mount Kilimanjaro will vanish in less than fifteen years.

It's February and it's cold in New York. That can help us believe
5   that the planet is not warming at a scary rate. But the snows are disappearing from Kilimanjaro.

A few years ago, a huge chunk of ice at the edge of Antarctica collapsed like a window shattered by a rock. Scientists were astonished. The piece had measured 48 miles by 22 miles and was
10 hundreds of feet thick. It sank into the ocean.

Many strange things are happening. The seasons are changing. Rainstorms are becoming more intense. Sea levels are rising. Mighty glaciers are shrinking. The permafrost—the *permanently* frozen soil of the Arctic and Antarctic—is thawing. Trees are flowering earlier.
15 Insects are coming out sooner.

Global warming is not coming. It's here.

There are likely to be some helpful results from the warming. Some areas will have longer growing seasons, more crops, fewer deaths from cold. But droughts, floods, heat waves, avalanches, and
20 tropical storms may cause disaster.

A report by the Intergovernmental Panel on Climate Change says that more people will be harmed than helped by climate change, even if average temperatures go up only a few degrees.

The report raises another important issue. Those most responsible
25 for global warming are not the most likely to be hurt by it.

For many years, the great industrial nations have used up natural resources. They have polluted the atmosphere with heat-trapping greenhouse gases.

But these nations have the wealth, technology, education, skills,
30 and systems to deal with global warming. Developing countries do not.

There is strong and growing evidence of the role of carbon dioxide and other greenhouse gases in global warming. Yet more and more of

---

"Rising Tides" by Bob Herbert adapted from *The New York Times,* February 22, 2001. Copyright © 2001 by **The New York Times Agency.** Retold by Holt, Rinehart and Winston. Reproduced by permission of the publisher.

these gases fill the atmosphere. Government leaders are not

35 responding to the problem fast enough.

Carbon dioxide doesn't just float away in a day or two. It stays in the atmosphere for more than a hundred years. The effects of our failure to act will last for centuries.

Americans have a special responsibility. The United States is the

40 mightiest nation on the planet. Our industrial pollution has added more to global warming than any other country's. To be fair to our neighbors and to future generations, we should make sacrifices.

But that's only one approach. Another is just to ignore the problem and go on feasting greedily at the table of the world's

45 resources. Why not? All you have to do is convince yourself that hurting the planet is somebody else's problem.

EVALUATING AN ARGUMENT

Herbert claims that governments are not responding to the problem of global warming fast enough (lines 34–35). Underline the facts in lines 36–38 that he presents as evidence for this claim.

EVALUATING AN ARGUMENT

Circle the loaded words Herbert uses in lines 43–46. Then, on the lines below, explain why you think he makes this emotional appeal.

_____

_____

_____

_____

_____

_____

_____

_____

_____

_____

Evaluating an Argument

When you **evaluate an argument,** first make sure you understand the claim, or point the writer is making. Then, identify the kinds of support the writer offers for his or her claim. Logical appeals include reasons and evidence—facts, statistics, examples, and expert opinions. Emotional appeals include loaded words and anecdotes.

Fill in the chart below with examples from "Rising Tides." One item has been filled in for you.

Evaluating an Author's Argument
Claim:

Logical Appeals
 	
Reason 1: Global warming is here now.
  Evidence: Ice caps are melting, rainstorms are more intense, sea levels are rising, glaciers are shrinking, permafrost is melting, trees flower earlier, and insects come out sooner.
 	
Reason 2:
  Evidence:
 	
Reason 3:
  Evidence:

Emotional Appeals Loaded words:

Vocabulary Development

Loaded Words

Words that are likely to cause an emotional response in the reader or listener are called **loaded words.** That is because they are loaded with a lot of feeling.

For each of the loaded words from "Rising Tides" listed below, describe your response—what you feel or think about when you hear the word. Then, write a sentence of your own using the word. One has been done for you.

1. pretend (line 1)

My response: _____

_____

My sentence: _____

_____

2. scary (line 5)

My response: _____

_____

My sentence: _____

_____

3. astonished (line 9)

My response: I think of a huge surprise—something very unexpected. It could be really good or really bad.

My sentence: I was astonished when I got an A on a test I thought I had failed.

_____

4. mightiest (line 40)

My response: _____

_____

My sentence: _____

_____

American History

Literary Focus: Biographical and Historical Approach

Many stories are based on the writers' life experiences. Names and details are changed, but these stories show something about the writers' childhood, heritage, or beliefs. This is called a **biographical approach.** When Judith Ortiz Cofer's family moved from Puerto Rico to Paterson, New Jersey, they lived in a large apartment house called El Building, much like Elena's home in the story you are about to read.

Sometimes the **themes** and issues of stories are also related to the **historical period** in which they take place. The historical period may be central to the story, or it may just be background for the characters' lives. The title "American History" tells you that the historical period will be important in this story.

Reading Skill: Summarizing

As you read a story, it is a good idea to pause every so often and summarize what is happening. When you **summarize,** you tell only the most important events. To figure out which events are important, think about the main characters and what happens to them.

Into the Story

President John F. Kennedy was killed on November 22, 1963, in Dallas, Texas. Just about any American living then can tell you where he or she was on that day. The date is a part of our national memory, much like September 11, 2001, when the World Trade Center buildings were destroyed. These tragic days have affected how we think of ourselves as a nation. In "American History," the narrator has another important reason to remember the day Kennedy died.

American History

BASED ON THE STORY BY

Judith Ortiz Cofer

It was a cold gray day in Paterson, and I was miserable. "Hey, Skinny Bones, pump it, girl." Gail yelled, "Didn't you eat your rice and beans and pork chops for breakfast today?"

5 I could not manage to coordinate the jump rope with Gail. The chill was entering my bones, making me cry, humiliating me. I hated the city, especially in winter. I hated Public School 13, and I hated my skinny, flat-chested body.

Seeing Eugene was the one source of beauty and light that school year. In August, Eugene and his family had moved into the only house 10 on the block that had a yard. I could see his kitchen and backyard from my window in El Building. Eugene was tall and blond, and he wore glasses. I liked him right away because he sat at the kitchen table and read books for hours.

Once school started, I looked for him in all my classes, but PS 15 13 was a huge crowded place. It took me days to discover that Eugene was in honors classes. These classes were not open to me because English was not my first language, though I was a straight-A student. After much skillful planning I managed to "run into him" in the hallway. One day I blurted out, "You're Eugene. Right?" I was 20 ready for rejection, but he smiled and nodded. In the following weeks, we walked home together.

My father had a good job at the bluejeans factory in Passaic and soon, he kept assuring us, we would be moving to a house there. Every Sunday we drove out to the suburbs where children 25 made snowmen from pure white snow, not like the gray slush of Paterson, which seemed to fall from the sky in that color. I listened to my parents' dreams, spoken in Spanish, like their stories about life in Puerto Rico before I was born. My dreams were about going to college and becoming a teacher.

30 Eugene's family had come from Georgia. The kids at school called him "the Hick" and made fun of the way he talked. "Skinny Bones and the Hick" was what they called us at school when we were seen together.

On the day that President Kennedy was shot, Mr. DePalma 35 asked us to line up in front of him. A short, muscular man with

slicked-down black hair, Mr. DePalma was the science teacher, PE coach, and disciplinarian at PS 13. We were shocked to see he was crying. Someone giggled behind me.

"Listen," Mr. DePalma said. His voice broke, and he covered

40 his face with his hands. "Listen," he repeated, "something awful has happened." There was a lot of laughter. Mr. DePalma shrieked, "The president is dead, you idiots. I should have known that wouldn't mean anything to a bunch of losers like you kids. Go home." No one moved for a minute; then we all scrambled madly to

45 get out of there.

As I headed home there was an eerie feeling on the streets. There were no horns blasting that day. There was a profound[1] silence in El Building, with no music spilling out from open doors. I found my mother sitting in front of our television set. She looked at

50 me with a tear-streaked face. I went into my room.

Though I wanted to feel the right thing about President Kennedy's death, I could not fight the elation[2] that stirred in my chest. Today I was to visit Eugene in his house. He had asked me to study for an American history test with him.

55 I got my books together. When I went in to tell my mother that I was going to a friend's house to study, I did not expect her reaction.

"You are going out *today*? The president has been killed. We must show respect. He was a great man. Come to church with me tonight." My first impulse was to comfort her because she seemed

60 so bewildered, but I had to meet Eugene.

"I have a test to study for, Mama. I will be home by eight," I said.

"You are forgetting who you are," Mama said. "I have seen you staring down at that boy's house. You are heading for humiliation

65 and pain." She spoke in Spanish in a resigned tone that surprised me, as if she did not intend to stop me from "heading for humiliation and pain."

I walked around the chain-link fence that separated El Building from Eugene's house. His door was painted deep green, *verde*—the

70 color of hope. Moments after my knock, the door opened a crack

---

1. **profound** (proh FOWND): deeply felt.
2. **elation** (ee LAY shuhn): a feeling of great happiness.

Here's HOW

VOCABULARY

I know that discipline is a way to enforce rules. So in line 37, I think *disciplinarian* means "someone who enforces the rules."

Your TURN

HISTORICAL APPROACH

How do people in the story react to President Kennedy's death? Underline the details in lines 37–50 on which you base your answer. Then, respond on the lines below.

_____

_____

_____

Your TURN

BIOGRAPHICAL APPROACH

Since this story is based in part on the writer's own experience, what kind of "humiliation and pain" (lines 64–65) do you think Elema's mother means that she is headed for?

_____

_____

_____

_____

_____

Here's HOW

Your TURN

SUMMARIZING

Summarize what happens from when Elena goes to Eugene's house (line 68) to the end of the story.

_____

_____

_____

_____

_____

_____

_____

_____

_____

_____

_____

_____

_____

and the red, swollen face of a woman appeared. She had a halo of red hair floating over a delicate white face.

"What do you want?" Her voice sounded sweet, as if drenched with honey, but her tone was not friendly.

75 "I'm Eugene's friend. He asked me over. To study." I said.

"You live there?" She pointed up to El Building, which looked like a gray prison.

"Yes. I do."

She looked intently at me for a couple of heartbeats, then said

80 as if to herself, "I don't know how you people do it." Then directly to me, she said, "Listen. Honey. Eugene doesn't want to study with you. He is a smart boy. Doesn't need help. You understand me. I am truly sorry if he said you could come over. He cannot study with you. It's nothing personal. You understand? We won't be in this

85 place much longer, no need for him to get close to people. It'll just make it harder for him later. Run back home now."

I stood there in shock.

"Didn't you hear what I said?" She seemed very angry, and I finally snapped out of my trance. As I turned away from the green

90 door I heard her close it gently.

That night I lay in my bed trying to feel the right thing for our dead president, but my tears were strictly for me. Sometime during the night, I went to my window and pressed my face to the glass. Looking up at the streetlight, I could see the white snow falling like a

95 lace veil over its face. I did not look down to see it turning gray as it touched the ground below.

Summarizing

When you **summarize** a story, you retell the main events in the order in which they happen. Use the chart below to summarize the main events in "American History." Some events have been filled in for you.

Event 1

Elena is teased at school for being Puerto Recan.

Event 2

Event 3

President Kennedy is shot

Event 4

Event 5

Elena goes to Engene's house to study.

Event 6

From the Odyssey, Part One

Literary Focus: Heroes

We all admire heroes in books and movies—and in real life, too. In fiction, as in real life, heroes often set out on a journey or quest to have adventures and accomplish great deeds. Heroic characters face **external conflicts**—struggles with other characters or with forces of nature. Epic heroes like Odysseus usually represent the values of their society. As you read about Odysseus, think about how he overcomes his conflicts. How is he heroic?

HELP WANTED

Epic Hero: Seeking experienced monster slayer. Must have superhuman powers. Good working relations with Greek gods helpful. Work history must reflect society's highest values. Travel and long hours will be required. No salary, but people will read about your adventures for centuries.

Reading Skill: Monitor Your Comprehension

As you read this **epic**—a long narrative poem that tells the great deeds of a hero—stop now and then to ask yourself questions. Ask:

- What has happened so far?
- Why did it happen?
- Where did it happen?
- What might happen next?
- Can I visualize, or picture, what is happening?
- What do I think of the characters and their decisions?
- What connections can I make between the poem and my life?

Into the Epic

The *Odyssey* is an epic poem about a soldier going home from war. It is considered one of the greatest adventure stories ever told. We credit a man named Homer with writing the poem, but the story was probably told earlier and passed along by wandering poets, who sang and recited stories for a living.

FROM THE

Odyssey

PART ONE

Homer

The Cyclops

YOU NEED TO KNOW In this adventure, Odysseus[1] describes his meeting with the Cyclops[2] named Polyphemus.[3] Polyphemus's father is Poseidon,[4] god of the sea. Out of curiosity, Odysseus and his men have entered the Cyclops's cave. They wait for Polyphemus to return to the cave, and they will have to be clever in order to escape.

'We lit a fire, burnt an offering,[5]

and took some cheese to eat; then sat in silence

around the embers, waiting. When he came

he had a load of dry boughs on his shoulder

5   to stoke his fire at suppertime. He dumped it

with a great crash into that hollow cave,

and we all scattered fast to the far wall.

Then over the broad cavern floor he ushered

the ewes he meant to milk. He left his rams

10 and he-goats in the yard outside, and swung

high overhead a slab of solid rock

to close the cave. Two dozen four-wheeled wagons,

with heaving wagon teams, could not have stirred

the tonnage of that rock from where he wedged it

15 over the doorsill. Next he took his seat

and milked his bleating ewes. A practiced job

he made of it, giving each ewe her suckling;[6]

thickened his milk, then, into curds and whey,[7]

---

1. **Odysseus** (oh DIHS ee uhs).
2. **Cyclops** (SY klahps): a race of giants with one eye in the center of their forehead.
3. **Polyphemus** (PAHL ih FEE muhs).
4. **Poseidon** (poh SY duhn).
5. **burnt an offering:** in ancient cultures, people often tried to please their gods by burning offerings of meat and other things.
6. **suckling:** a young animal still feeding on its mother's milk.
7. **curds and whey:** curds are the thick lumps of soured milk used to make cheese; whey is the watery liquid that is left. Polyphemus makes cheese, which is why Odysseus and his men have cheese to eat in line 2.

From Books IX "New Coasts and Poseidon's Son," XVI "Father and Son," XXII "Death in the Great Hall," and XXIII "The Trunk of the Olive Tree" from *Homer: The Odyssey;* translated by Robert Fitzgerald. Copyright © 1961, 1963 by Robert Fitzgerald; copyright renewed © 1989 by Benedict R. C. Fitzgerald. Reproduced by permission of **Farrar, Straus & Giroux, LLC.**

Here's HOW

MONITOR YOUR COMPREHENSION

I wonder who the *he* is in line 3. I learned from You Need to Know that Odysseus and his men are waiting for the Cyclops Polyphemus. *He* must be Polyphemus.

Here's HOW

VOCABULARY

I've seen the word *ewes* (yooz) in line 9 before, but I can't remember exactly what they are. The poem says the Cyclops is going to milk them, and the next sentence mentions rams. I'm pretty sure *ewes* are female sheep.

Your TURN

MONITOR YOUR COMPREHENSION

What has happened in lines 10–12 that will make it hard for Odysseus and his men to escape from the cave?

_____

_____

_____

_____

_____

_____

sieved out the curds to drip in withy baskets,[8]

20 and poured the whey to stand in bowls

cooling until he drank it for his supper.

When all these chores were done, he poked the fire,

heaping on brushwood. In the glare he saw us.

'Strangers,' he said, 'who are you? And where from?

25 What brings you here by seaways—a fair traffic?

Or are you wandering rogues, who cast your lives

like dice, and ravage other folk by sea?'

We felt a pressure on our hearts, in dread

of that deep rumble and that mighty man.

30 But all the same I spoke up in reply:

'We are from Troy, Achaeans,[9] blown off course

by shifting gales on the Great South Sea;

homeward bound, but taking routes and ways

uncommon; so the will of Zeus would have it.

35 We served under Agamemnon, son of Atreus[10]—

the whole world knows what city

he laid waste, what armies he destroyed.

It was our luck to come here; here we stand,

beholden for your help, or any gifts

40 you give—as custom is to honor strangers.

We would entreat[11] you, great Sir, have a care

for the gods' courtesy; Zeus will avenge

the unoffending guest.'

IN OTHER WORDS Polyphemus enters the cave where Odysseus and his men are waiting. Polyphemus rolls a huge rock over the cave opening, then milks his sheep and starts to make his supper. Finally, Polyphemus sees the soldiers and asks them who they are. Odysseus explains that

---

8. **withy baskets:** baskets made from willow twigs.
9. **Achaeans** (uh KEE uhnz): Greeks.
10. **Agamemnon** (AG uh MEM NAHN); **Atreus** (AY tree uhs).
11. **entreat:** ask or beg.

VOCABULARY

I know that a *sieve* (sihv) is a strainer that separates larger pieces out of a mixture, like tea leaves out of tea. So *sieved* in line 19 must mean strained, or separated.

VOCABULARY

In lines 24–27, the Cyclops is asking what kind of men these are in his cave. Underline the words that help you know what *rogues* are.

VOCABULARY

You've probably seen the word *ravage* before. Read lines 24–27 again. Then, write what you think *ravage* means on the lines below.

_____

_____

_____

_____

VOCABULARY

In line 32, I can tell *gales* means "strong winds" because Odysseus says they were blown off course.

VOCABULARY

In line 46, I can tell that *Cyclopes* (SY klohps) is the plural form of *Cyclops*.

Here's HOW

HEROES

Usually I don't think of lying as heroic, but Odysseus just found out that the Cyclops doesn't fear the gods, so he is probably smart not to trust him. Cleverness could be a heroic quality. Maybe it is one that was admired by the ancient Greeks.

MONITOR YOUR COMPREHENSION

I can really picture the scene described in lines 60–65, and it's horrible! The comparison of the soldiers to squirming puppies and of the eating Cyclops to a crunching mountain lion and the other details help me visualize the awful scene.

he and his men are soldiers who fought in the attack on Troy. Now they are heading home but got lost along the way. Odysseus reminds the Cyclops that Zeus, king of the gods, will punish anyone who mistreats strangers.

He answered this
from his brute chest, unmoved:
‘You are a ninny,

45 or else you come from the other end of nowhere,
telling me, mind the gods! We Cyclops
care not a whistle for your thundering Zeus
or all the gods in bliss; we have more force by far.
I would not let you go for fear of Zeus—

50 you or your friends—unless I had a whim to.
Tell me, where was it, now, you left your ship—
around the point, or down the shore, I wonder?’

He thought he'd find out, but I saw through this,
and answered with a ready lie:
‘My ship?

55 Poseidon Lord, who sets the earth atremble,
broke it up on the rocks at your land's end.
A wind from seaward served him, drove us there.
We are survivors, these good men and I.’

IN OTHER WORDS The Cyclops answers that he is not afraid of any god. Then he asks where they left their ship. Odysseus lies, saying that the ship was smashed to pieces on the rocks.

Neither reply nor pity came from him,

60 but in one stride he clutched at my companions
and caught two in his hands like squirming puppies
to beat their brains out, spattering the floor.
Then he dismembered them and made his meal,
gaping and crunching like a mountain lion—

65 everything: innards, flesh, and marrow bones.

We cried aloud, lifting our hands to Zeus,
powerless, looking on at this, appalled;
but Cyclops went on filling up his belly
with manflesh and great gulps of whey,
70 then lay down like a mast[12] among his sheep.

IN OTHER WORDS Suddenly, the Cyclops grabs two soldiers, kills them, and eats them. Odysseus and his men watch in horror. Stomach full, the monster lies down to sleep.

My heart beat high now at the chance of action,
and drawing the sharp sword from my hip I went
along his flank[13] to stab him where the midriff
holds the liver. I had touched the spot
75 when sudden fear stayed me: if I killed him
we perished there as well, for we could never
move his ponderous[14] doorway slab aside.
So we were left to groan and wait for morning.

IN OTHER WORDS Odysseus pulls out his sword, ready to kill the sleeping Cyclops. Then he remembers the slab of solid rock that closes the door of the cave. Only the Cyclops is strong enough to move that rock. They are trapped in the cave. If the Cyclops dies, they all die.

When the young Dawn with fingertips of rose
80 lit up the world, the Cyclops built a fire
and milked his handsome ewes, all in due order,
putting the sucklings to the mothers. Then,
his chores being all dispatched, he caught
another brace of men to make his breakfast,
85 and whisked away his great door slab
to let his sheep go through—but he, behind,

---

12. **mast:** a tall pole that supports the sails on a ship.
13. **flank:** on the side, between ribs and hip.
14. **ponderous:** heavy.

Here's HOW

VOCABULARY

In line 67, *appalled* must mean something like "horrified." That's how the scene makes me feel, so I think that must be what it means.

Here's HOW

HEROES

Odysseus sounds like a brave hero who wants to fight when he draws his sword. He also shows his cleverness by realizing that if he kills the Cyclops while the boulder is still blocking the entrance, they won't be able to get out.

Here's HOW

VOCABULARY

In line 84, a *brace of men* sounds weird. I checked my dictionary, and there were lots of meanings. The only one that makes sense is "a pair." So I guess the Cyclops ate two more of Odysseus' buddies.

reset the stone as one would cap a quiver.[15]

There was a din of whistling as the Cyclops

rounded his flock to higher ground, then stillness.

90 And now I pondered how to hurt him worst,

if but Athena[16] granted what I prayed for.

Here are the means I thought would serve my turn:[17]

a club, or staff, lay there along the fold—

an olive tree, felled green and left to season

95 for Cyclops' hand. And it was like a mast

a lugger[18] of twenty oars, broad in the beam—

a deep-seagoing craft—might carry:

so long, so big around, it seemed. Now I

chopped out a six-foot section of this pole

100 and set it down before my men, who scraped it;

and when they had it smooth, I hewed[19] again

to make a stake with pointed end. I held this

in the fire's heart and turned it, toughening it,

then hid it, well back in the cavern, under

105 one of the dung piles in profusion there.

Now came the time to toss for it: who ventured

along with me? Whose hand could bear to thrust

and grind that spike in Cyclops's eye, when mild

sleep had mastered him? As luck would have it,

110 the men I would have chosen won the toss—

four strong men, and I made five as captain.

IN OTHER WORDS   In the morning, the Cyclops gobbles two more of the men for breakfast. Then he takes his sheep out to pasture, sealing the cave behind him. Trapped again, Odysseus looks for a weapon. He finds a giant log, which he and his men sharpen to a spike. They will jab it in the Cyclops's eye.

15. **quiver:** a long, narrow container for arrows.
16. **Athena** (uh THEE nuh): goddess of wisdom and the arts of war and peace.
17. **means I thought would serve my turn:** items that would help me.
18. **lugger:** a type of sailboat.
19. **hewed:** chopped and cut.

At evening came the shepherd with his flock,

his woolly flock. The rams as well, this time,

entered the cave: by some sheepherding whim[20]—

115 or a god's bidding—none were left outside.

He hefted his great boulder into place

and sat him down to milk the bleating ewes

in proper order, put the lambs to suck,

and swiftly ran through all his evening chores.

120 Then he caught two more men and feasted on them.

My moment was at hand, and I went forward

holding an ivy bowl of my dark drink,

looking up, saying:

        'Cyclops, try some wine.

Here's liquor to wash down your scraps of men.

125 Taste it, and see the kind of drink we carried

under our planks. I meant it for an offering

if you would help us home. But you are mad,

unbearable, a bloody monster! After this,

will any other traveler come to see you?'

130 He seized and drained the bowl, and it went down

so fiery and smooth he called for more:

        'Give me another, thank you kindly. Tell me,

how are you called? I'll make a gift will please you.

Even Cyclopes know the wine grapes grow

135 out of grassland and loam in heaven's rain,

but here's a bit of nectar and ambrosia!'

Three bowls I brought him, and he poured them down.

I saw the fuddle and flush come over him,

then I sang out in cordial tones:

---

20. **whim:** sudden desire.

HEROES

Odysseus is being clever in lines 123–129. I think he's going to make the Cyclops sleepy by giving him wine.

Your TURN

VOCABULARY

The Cyclops seems to like the wine. What do you think he means in line 136 when he calls it "nectar and ambrosia"?

_____

_____

_____

_____

_____

_____

VOCABULARY

The Cyclops has had quite a bit of liquor now. I think *fuddle and flush* in line 138 means he is turning red and looking confused, as if he's drunk.

'Cyclops,

140   you ask my honorable name? Remember
the gift you promised me, and I shall tell you.
My name is Nohbdy: mother, father, and friends,
everyone calls me Nohbdy.'

And he said:

'Nohbdy's my meat, then, after I eat his friends.
145   Others come first. There's a noble gift, now.'

IN OTHER WORDS   Evening comes, and the Cyclops returns with his flock of sheep. He eats two more men for his dinner. Then Odysseus offers him wine. Pleased with the wine, the Cyclops asks Odysseus his name. Odysseus says he is called "Nohbdy."

Even as he spoke, he reeled and tumbled backward,
his great head lolling to one side; and sleep
took him like any creature. Drunk, hiccuping,
he dribbled streams of liquor and bits of men.

150   Now, by the gods, I drove my big hand spike
deep in the embers, charring it again,
and cheered my men along with battle talk
to keep their courage up: no quitting now.
The pike of olive, green though it had been,
155   reddened and glowed as if about to catch.
I drew it from the coals and my four fellows
gave me a hand, lugging it near the Cyclops
as more than natural force nerved them; straight
forward they sprinted, lifted it, and rammed it
160   deep in his crater eye, and I leaned on it
turning it as a shipwright turns a drill
in planking, having men below to swing
the two-handled strap that spins it in the groove.
So with our brand we bored that great eye socket
165   while blood ran out around the red-hot bar.

Eyelid and lash were seared; the pierced ball
hissed broiling, and the roots popped.

In a smithy[21]
one sees a white-hot axhead or an adze[22]
plunged and wrung in a cold tub, screeching steam—
170 the way they make soft iron hale and hard—
just so that eyeball hissed around the spike.
The Cyclops bellowed and the rock roared round him,
and we fell back in fear. Clawing his face
he tugged the bloody spike out of his eye,
175 threw it away, and his wild hands went groping;
then he set up a howl for Cyclopes
who lived in caves on windy peaks nearby.
Some heard him; and they came by divers[23] ways
to clump around outside and call:

'What ails you,
180 Polyphemus? Why do you cry so sore
in the starry night? You will not let us sleep.
Sure no man's driving off your flock? No man
has tricked you, ruined you?'

IN OTHER WORDS The drunken Cyclops falls asleep.
Odysseus and his men push their giant spike into the fire
until it is red-hot. Then, with the help of four men, Odysseus
drives the spike into the sleeping monster's eye. The Cyclops
awakens, roaring in pain. Hearing his howls, other Cyclopes
leave their caves and come to find out what is wrong.

Out of the cave
the mammoth[24] Polyphemus roared in answer:

185 'Nohbdy, Nohbdy's tricked me. Nohbdy's ruined me!'

---

21. **smithy:** blacksmith's shop, where iron tools are made.
22. **adze:** tool like an ax but with a longer, curved blade.
23. **divers:** diverse; various.
24. **mammoth:** huge.

Here's
HOW

VOCABULARY

I thought *hale* in line 170 meant "healthy," but how can iron be made healthy? I checked the dictionary, and I was right, but it also says "sound in body." I guess *hale* is a figure of speech. I think it's called *personification* when you give an object human qualities.

Your
TURN

MONITOR YOUR COMPREHENSION

In lines 172–177, underline the details that help you visualize the Cyclops's reaction to what Odysseus and his men have done to him.

VOCABULARY

What do you think *sage* means
in line 186? Write your answer
on the lines below. Check a
dictionary to see if you're right.

_____

_____

HEROES

Re-read lines 204–214. What
heroic action is Odysseus
taking?

_____

_____

_____

_____

_____

_____

_____

_____

_____

To this rough shout they made a sage reply:

'Ah well, if nobody has played you foul
there in your lonely bed, we are no use in pain
given by great Zeus. Let it be your father,
Poseidon Lord, to whom you pray.'

190   So saying
they trailed away. And I was filled with laughter
to see how like a charm the name deceived them.
Now Cyclops, wheezing as the pain came on him,
fumbled to wrench away the great doorstone
195 and squatted in the breach[25] with arms thrown wide
for any silly beast or man who bolted—
hoping somehow I might be such a fool.
But I kept thinking how to win the game:
death sat there huge; how could we slip away?
200 I drew on all my wits, and ran through tactics,
reasoning as a man will for dear life,
until a trick came—and it pleased me well.
The Cyclops's rams were handsome, fat, with heavy
fleeces, a dark violet.

                                          Three abreast
205 I tied them silently together, twining
cords of willow from the ogre's bed;
then slung a man under each middle one
to ride there safely, shielded left and right.
So three sheep could convey each man. I took
210 the woolliest ram, the choicest of the flock,
and hung myself under his kinky belly,
pulled up tight, with fingers twisted deep
in sheepskin ringlets for an iron grip.
So, breathing hard, we waited until morning.

---

25. breach: opening.

IN OTHER WORDS Polyphemus cries out that "Nohbdy" has hurt him. The other Cyclopes reply that if nobody has hurt him, there is nothing they can do to help; and so they leave. Odysseus laughs to see how well his trick has worked. But they are still trapped. Polyphemus pushes the stone away and squats in the open doorway of the cave, hoping to catch the men trying to escape. Odysseus thinks up a plan of escape. He ties the sheep together in threes, then ties a man under each middle sheep. He hides himself under the Cyclops's best ram. They wait for morning.

215　When Dawn spread out her fingertips of rose
　　　the rams began to stir, moving for pasture,
　　　and peals of bleating echoed round the pens
　　　where dams with udders full called for a milking.
　　　Blinded, and sick with pain from his head wound,
220　the master stroked each ram, then let it pass,
　　　but my men riding on the pectoral fleece[26]
　　　the giant's blind hands blundering never found.
　　　Last of them all my ram, the leader, came,
　　　weighted by wool and me with my meditations.
225　The Cyclops patted him, and then he said:

　　　'Sweet cousin ram, why lag behind the rest
　　　in the night cave? You never linger so,
　　　but graze before them all, and go afar
　　　to crop sweet grass, and take your stately way
230　leading along the streams, until at evening
　　　you run to be the first one in the fold.
　　　Why, now, so far behind? Can you be grieving
　　　over your Master's eye? That carrion rogue[27]
　　　and his accurst companions burnt it out
235　when he had conquered all my wits with wine.
　　　Nohbdy will not get out alive, I swear.
　　　Oh, had you brain and voice to tell

---

26. **pectoral fleece:** wool on an animal's chest.
27. **carrion rogue:** rotten scoundrel. Carrion is decaying flesh.

Here's HOW

VOCABULARY

I've never seen the word *dam* used like it is in line 218, so I looked it up in my dictionary. The way it's used here, a *dam* is a "mother of a four-legged animal."

Your TURN

MONITOR YOUR COMPREHENSION

Re-read lines 226–233. What connection to your own life can you make to the affection the Cyclops shows to his best ram?

_____
_____
_____
_____
_____
_____
_____
_____
_____
_____
_____
_____
_____
_____
_____
_____
_____

Your TURN

VOCABULARY

What do you think an *adversary* is in line 257? Write your definition on the lines below. Now, check a dictionary to make sure you're right.

_____

_____

_____

_____

Your TURN

HEROES

Odysseus acted heroically by letting all his men escape from the cave before him. How does he again show his leadership in lines 251–255?

_____

_____

_____

_____

_____

_____

_____

_____

_____

_____

where he may be now, dodging all my fury!
Bashed by this hand and bashed on this rock wall
240 his brains would strew the floor, and I should have
rest from the outrage Nohbdy worked upon me.'

He sent us into the open, then. Close by,
I dropped and rolled clear of the ram's belly,
going this way and that to untie the men.
245 With many glances back, we rounded up
his fat, stiff-legged sheep to take aboard,
and drove them down to where the good ship lay.
We saw, as we came near, our fellows' faces
shining; then we saw them turn to grief
250 tallying those who had not fled from death.
I hushed them, jerking head and eyebrows up,
and in a low voice told them: 'Load this herd;
move fast, and put the ship's head toward the breakers.'
They all pitched in at loading, then embarked
255 and struck their oars into the sea. Far out,
as far offshore as shouted words would carry,
I sent a few back to the adversary:

IN OTHER WORDS   In the morning blind Polyphemus lets his sheep out. He touches each one as it passes, but the men are safely hidden. As the last ram goes by, with Odysseus hanging beneath, Polyphemus swears to destroy "Nohbdy." Free at last, the men run for their ship, taking the sheep with them. The rest of the crew is waiting. Quickly, they load the sheep on board and begin to row away.

'O Cyclops! Would you feast on my companions?
Puny, am I, in a Caveman's hands?
260 How do you like the beating that we gave you,
you damned cannibal? Eater of guests
under your roof! Zeus and the gods have paid you!'

The blind thing in his doubled fury broke
a hilltop in his hands and heaved it after us.
265 Ahead of our black prow it struck and sank
whelmed in a spuming geyser, a giant wave
that washed the ship stern foremost back to shore.
I got the longest boathook out and stood
fending us off, with furious nods to all
270 to put their backs into a racing stroke—
row, row or perish. So the long oars bent
kicking the foam sternward, making head
until we drew away, and twice as far.
Now when I cupped my hands I heard the crew
in low voices protesting:

275   'Godsake, Captain!
Why bait the beast again? Let him alone!'

'That tidal wave he made on the first throw
all but beached us.'

                         'All but stove[28] us in!'

'Give him our bearing[29] with your trumpeting,
he'll get the range and lob[30] a boulder.'

280   'Aye
He'll smash our timbers and our heads together!'

I would not heed them in my glorying spirit,
but let my anger flare and yelled:

                                 'Cyclops,
if ever mortal man inquire
285 how you were put to shame and blinded, tell him

---

28. **stove:** past participle of *stave*, meaning "to smash or break up."
29. **bearing:** location.
30. **lob:** toss.

Your
TURN

HEROES

Re-read lines 282–287. What do these lines tell you about Odysseus? Does this fit your idea of a hero? Why or why not?

Odysseus, raider of cities, took your eye:
Laertes'[31] son, whose home's on Ithaca!'

IN OTHER WORDS   Odysseus shouts at Polyphemus,
taunting him with their escape. Enraged, the Cyclops breaks
off a hilltop and throws it at the ship. The hilltop falls in the
water ahead of them, making a giant wave that pushes them
back to shore. The men row away again with all their might.
The men beg Odysseus to leave the Cyclops alone. But
Odysseus calls out to the Cyclops again, telling him his real
name.

At this he gave a mighty sob and rumbled:

'Now comes the weird[32] upon me, spoken of old.
290　A wizard, grand and wondrous, lived here—Telemus,[33]
a son of Eurymus;[34] great length of days
he had in wizardry among the Cyclopes,
and these things he foretold for time to come:
my great eye lost, and at Odysseus' hands.
295　Always I had in mind some giant, armed
in giant force, would come against me here.
But this, but you—small, pitiful, and twiggy—
you put me down with wine, you blinded me.
Come back, Odysseus, and I'll treat you well,
300　praying the god of earthquake to befriend you—
his son I am, for he by his avowal[35]
fathered me, and, if he will, he may
heal me of this black wound—he and no other
of all the happy gods or mortal men.'

305　Few words I shouted in reply to him:

---

31. **Laertes** (lay UHR teez).
32. **weird:** fate.
33. **Telemus** (TEHL uh muhs).
34. **Eurymus** (YOO ruh muhs).
35. **avowal:** a public announcement or acknowledgment; a proclamation.

'If I could take your life I would and take
your time away, and hurl you down to hell!
The god of earthquake could not heal you there!'

At this he stretched his hands out in his darkness
310 toward the sky of stars, and prayed Poseidon:

'O hear me, lord, blue girdler of the islands,[36]
if I am thine indeed, and thou art father:
grant that Odysseus, raider of cities, never
see his home: Laertes' son, I mean,
315 who kept his hall on Ithaca. Should destiny
intend that he shall see his roof again
among his family in his fatherland,
far be that day, and dark the years between.
Let him lose all companions, and return
320 under strange sail to bitter days at home.' . . ."

(*from* Book 9)

Your TURN

MONITOR YOUR COMPREHENSION

What is the result of Odysseus's taunting of the Cyclops? How do you predict the rest of Odysseus's journey will go? Will it be easy or full of grief?

_____

_____

_____

_____

_____

IN OTHER WORDS   Long ago, a wizard said that Polyphemus would be blinded by Odysseus. Hearing this name, the Cyclops realizes that his fate has come to pass. He asks Odysseus to come back, saying that he is the son of the god Poseidon, and that he will ask his father to treat Odysseus well. Odysseus responds with threats and insults. Polyphemus calls out to Poseidon, begging him to make sure that Odysseus never reaches home. Or, if that is impossible, to make his journey long and hard, and his final return full of grief.

---

36. **blue girdler of the islands:** a reference to the sea, which girdles, or surrounds, the islands. Poseidon is god of the sea.

Heroes

Today we use the word *hero* to describe many types of people we admire. Firefighters, police officers, and soldiers are often called heroes. A hero can also be a parent who makes sacrifices for a child, or someone who does an unglamorous job as if a lot depended on it.

Who are your heroes? Think about real people and fictional characters you admire. Select one, and compare his or her characteristics with those of Odysseus. Put a check mark next to characteristics that apply to Odysseus, your hero, or both. You can add characteristics at the bottom of the table if you'd like. One item is filled in for you.

Heroic Characteristics	Odysseus	My Hero: _____
Strong	✔	
Attractive		
Proud		
Adventurous		
Helpful		
Has enemies		
Gets magical help		
Clever		
Merciful		

Vocabulary Development

Synonyms

Draw a line connecting each word from "The Cyclops" listed in the left-hand column with the word or phrase in the right-hand column that means the same thing. The first one has been done for you.

1.	sieve	a.	horrified
2.	rogues	b.	wise
3.	ravage	c.	large amount
4.	gales	d.	opponent
5.	appalled	e.	strainer
6.	din	f.	strong winds
7.	profusion	g.	loud noise
8.	hale	h.	rascals
9.	sage	i.	destroy
10.	adversary	j.	healthy

From the Odyssey, Part Two

Literary Focus: Living Characters

Odysseus is brave and clever. The Cyclops is cruel and monstrous. Homer describes his characters with bold, powerful strokes. If you want to discover how storytellers reveal **character traits,** look at:

- **What the characters say or think**
- **What the characters do**
- **What other characters say about them**
- **How they are described**

As you read, think about what this information tells you. Are the characters noble or evil? wise or foolish? proud or humble? Or are they, like most real people, a combination of good and bad traits?

Reading Skill: Monitor Your Comprehension

To be sure you understand what you read, stop along the way and ask yourself questions. Ask the *5W-How?* questions: who? what? when? where? why? how? Then, try to visualize, or picture, what is happening; evaluate the character's actions and decisions; and make connections to your own experiences and prior knowledge.

Into the Epic

In Part Two of the Odyssey, Odysseus comes home after twenty years. You'll read about his meeting with his son, Telemachus; about his dealings with the men trying to marry his wife; and, finally, about his meeting with his faithful wife, Penelope.

FROM THE

Odyssey

PART TWO

Homer

The Meeting of Father and Son

But there were two men in the mountain hut—
Odysseus and the swineherd. At first light
blowing their fire up, they cooked their breakfast
and sent their lads out, driving herds to root
in the tall timber.

5   When Telemachus[1] came,
the wolfish troop of watchdogs only fawned on him
as he advanced. Odysseus heard them go
and heard the light crunch of a man's footfall—
at which he turned quickly to say:

                    "Eumaeus,[2]
10 here is one of your crew come back, or maybe
another friend: the dogs are out there snuffling
belly down; not one has even growled.
I can hear footsteps—"

                But before he finished
his tall son stood at the door.

                The swineherd
15 rose in surprise, letting a bowl and jug
tumble from his fingers. Going forward,

---

1. **Telemachus** (tuh LEHM uh kuhs): Odysseus' son.
2. **Eumaeus** (yoo MEE uhs): a swineherd. One of Odysseus' servants.

Sidebar:

Here's HOW

VOCABULARY

I know that a group of soldiers is called a troop. So *troop* in line 6 must mean "group."

Here's HOW

VOCABULARY

Line 6 says the dogs "only fawned on him." The word *only* makes me think the dogs didn't bark or attack, even though they're watchdogs. So *fawned* must mean the dogs acted friendly. They probably wagged their tails and licked his hands.

Here's HOW

LIVING CHARACTERS

I haven't even met Telemachus yet, but I like him. That's because the dogs like him, and I trust dogs.

Your TURN

VOCABULARY

Re-read lines 10–13. What do you think *snuffling* means in line 11? Underline words around *snuffling* that help you understand what it means.

_____

_____

_____

_____

he kissed the young man's head, his shining eyes

and both hands, while his own tears brimmed and fell.

Think of a man whose dear and only son,

20 born to him in exile, reared with labor,

has lived ten years abroad and now returns:

how would that man embrace his son! Just so

the herdsman clapped his arms around Telemachus

and covered him with kisses—for he knew

25 the lad had got away from death. He said:

"Light of my days, Telemachus,

you made it back! When you took ship for Pylos[3]

I never thought to see you here again.

Come in, dear child, and let me feast my eyes;

30 here you are, home from the distant places!

How rarely, anyway, you visit us,

your own men, and your own woods and pastures!

Always in the town, a man would think

you loved the suitors'[4] company, those dogs!"

IN OTHER WORDS Telemachus arrives unexpectedly. The swineherd is very glad to see the young man, who has been gone a long time. Telemachus had sailed to the island of Pylos looking for news of his father.

35 Telemachus with his clear candor[5] said:

"I am with you, Uncle.[6] See now, I have come

because I wanted to see you first, to hear from you

if Mother stayed at home—or is she married

off to someone, and Odysseus' bed

40 left empty for some gloomy spider's weaving?"

---

3. **Pylos:** home of Nestor, one of Odysseus' fellow soldiers. Telemachus had gone to see if Nestor knew anything about Odysseus.
4. **suitors:** group of men who ate up Odysseus' food and tried to marry his wife, Penelope, while he was away.
5. **candor:** plain-spoken honesty.
6. **Uncle:** here, a term of affection.

Here's HOW

VOCABULARY

I've looked up *exile* (line 20) before. I know that it means "living in a foreign country." Even if I didn't know the word, the phrase "has lived ten years abroad" in line 21 gives me a good clue.

Here's HOW

MONITOR YOUR COMPREHENSION

In lines 19–22, Homer asks me directly to make a connection to my own experience, just like my teachers say I should do when I read. At first I was confused, though, and thought he was talking about Odysseus. But Odysseus was away for twenty years, not ten. I think the poet is talking about the swineherd. So I guess I'm just supposed to think about how *anyone* whose son has been gone for ten years would feel when he returned. If I were away from my dad that long, I'd sure be glad to see him again!

Your TURN

LIVING CHARACTERS

What do you think of someone who speaks with candor, or plain-spoken honesty (line 35)?

_____

_____

_____

_____

Here's
HOW

MONITOR YOUR COMPREHENSION

I figure a *forester* (line 41) is someone who works in the forest. But I thought a swineherd was someone who keeps pigs. Maybe in those days, instead of keeping the pigs in a pen and feeding them, they took them into the forest to find their own food.

Your
TURN

VOCABULARY

Have you ever heard the terms *check* and *checkmate* used in chess? Based on the meaning of those words, what do you think Telemachus did in line 48?

_____

_____

_____

Your
TURN

LIVING CHARACTERS

Odysseus, who is dressed like a beggar, gets up to offer his seat to Telemachus. Telemachus tells him to sit down (line 49). What does this behavior tell you about Telemachus?

_____

_____

_____

Gently the forester replied to this:

"At home indeed your mother is, poor lady
still in the women's hall. Her nights and days
are wearied out with grieving."

                                    Stepping back
45 he took the bronze-shod lance, and the young prince
entered the cabin over the worn door stone.
Odysseus moved aside, yielding his couch,
but from across the room Telemachus checked him:

IN OTHER WORDS Telemachus explains that he came here first to get news of his mother, Penelope. Has she remarried? No, says the swineherd. She stays at home, still grieving day and night for Odysseus.

"Friend, sit down; we'll find another chair
50 in our own hut. Here is the man to make one!"

The swineherd, when the quiet man sank down,
built a new pile of evergreens and fleeces—
a couch for the dear son of great Odysseus—
then gave them trenchers[7] of good meat, left over
55 from the roast pork of yesterday, and heaped up
willow baskets full of bread, and mixed
an ivy bowl of honey-hearted wine.
Then he in turn sat down, facing Odysseus,
their hands went out upon the meat and drink
60 as they fell to,[8] ridding themselves of hunger. . . .

IN OTHER WORDS Telemachus does not recognize his father, who wears rags like a beggar. The three men sit down for a meal together.

---

7. **trenchers:** wooden platters.
8. **fell to:** went about the task, in this case, eating.

Here's HOW

LIVING CHARACTERS

When we read "The Cyclops," we learned that Odysseus was an epic hero, but in this story, when Odysseus was dressed like a beggar, he wasn't acting very heroic. Now, in lines 61–65, the goddess Athena is making him look heroic. He must be a great hero for a goddess to do that for him.

Your TURN

LIVING CHARACTERS

Circle the words Homer uses to describe Odysseus in line 75.

Your TURN

MONITOR YOUR COMPREHENSION

An old beggar suddenly turns into a handsome younger man who embraces Telemachus and tells him he is the father Telemachus hasn't seen in twenty years. If you were Telemachus, how would you react?

_____

_____

_____

_____

_____

_____

YOU NEED TO KNOW After eating, the swineherd leaves to tell Penelope that her son has returned. Odysseus leaves the room and is transformed by the goddess Athena.

. . . She[9] tipped her golden wand upon the man,
making his cloak pure white, and the knit tunic
fresh around him. Lithe[10] and young she made him,
ruddy with sun, his jawline clean, the beard

65 no longer gray upon his chin. And she
withdrew when she had done.
                         Then Lord Odysseus
reappeared—and his son was thunderstruck.
Fear in his eyes, he looked down and away
as though it were a god, and whispered:
                                    "Stranger,

70 you are no longer what you were just now!
Your cloak is new; even your skin! You are
one of the gods who rule the sweep of heaven!
Be kind to us, we'll make you fair oblation[11]
and gifts of hammered gold. Have mercy on us!"

75 The noble and enduring man replied:

"No god. Why take me for a god? No, no.
I am that father whom your boyhood lacked
and suffered pain for lack of. I am he."

Held back too long, the tears ran down his cheeks
as he embraced his son.

80   Only Telemachus,
uncomprehending, wild
with incredulity,[12] cried out:
                             "You cannot
be my father Odysseus! Meddling spirits

---

9. **She:** Athena.
10. **Lithe** (*lyth*): limber.
11. **oblation** (ahb LAY shuhn): offering of a sacrifice. Telemachus thinks the stranger (his father) is a god.
12. **incredulity** (IHN kruh DOO luh tee): disbelief.

Your TURN

LIVING CHARACTERS

Finish reading this page. Does Odysseus act here like a great hero, like an ordinary father, or both? Underline details in the poem that support your opinion. Then, write your response on the lines below.

_____

_____

_____

_____

_____

_____

_____

_____

_____

_____

_____

_____

_____

_____

_____

_____

_____

_____

_____

_____

_____

_____

_____

conceived this trick to twist the knife in me!

85 No man of woman born could work these wonders

by his own craft, unless a god came into it

with ease to turn him young or old at will.

I swear you were in rags and old,

and here you stand like one of the immortals!"

90 Odysseus brought his ranging mind to bear

and said:

        "This is not princely, to be swept

away by wonder at your father's presence.

No other Odysseus will ever come,

for he and I are one, the same; his bitter

95 fortune and his wanderings are mine.

Twenty years gone, and I am back again

on my own island. . . ."

                Then, throwing

his arms around this marvel of a father,

Telemachus began to weep. Salt tears

100 rose from the wells of longing in both men,

and cries burst from both as keen and fluttering

as those of the great taloned hawk,

whose nestlings[13] farmers take before they fly.

So helplessly they cried, pouring out tears,

105 and might have gone on weeping so till sundown. . . .

             (_from_ Book 16)

IN OTHER WORDS   The swineherd goes to tell Penelope her son has returned. Now Athena waves her wand, making Odysseus look like himself again. Telemachus is shocked by the change and thinks his father is a god in disguise. Odysseus throws his arms around his son and says he is not a god, but his long-lost father. Finally persuaded, Telemachus hugs Odysseus and they cry with joy.

---

13. nestlings: young birds that are not ready to leave the nest.

Death at the Palace

YOU NEED TO KNOW After rejoining Telemachus,
Odysseus prepares to take revenge on the suitors. The suitors
have stolen items from his house, misused his servants, and
tried to marry his wife. Disguised again as a beggar, Odysseus
joins the suitors in a festive archery competition.

Now shrugging off his rags the wiliest[1] fighter of the
islands
leapt and stood on the broad doorsill, his own bow in his
hand.
He poured out at his feet a rain of arrows from the quiver
and spoke to the crowd:

"So much for that. Your clean-cut game is over.
5 Now watch me hit a target that no man has hit before,
if I can make this shot. Help me, Apollo."[2]

He drew to his fist the cruel head of an arrow for
Antinous[3]
just as the young man leaned to lift his beautiful
drinking cup,
embossed,[4] two-handled, golden: the cup was in his
fingers,
the wine was even at his lips, and did he dream of
10 death?
How could he? In that revelry amid his throng of friends
who would imagine a single foe—though a strong foe
indeed—
could dare to bring death's pain on him and darkness on
his eyes?
Odysseus' arrow hit him under the chin
15 and punched up to the feathers through his throat.

---

1. **wiliest:** craftiest; cleverest.
2. **"Help me, Apollo.":** Odysseus prays to Apollo because this day is one of the god's feast
   days. Apollo is also the god of archery.
3. **Antinous** (an TIHN oh uhs): leader of the suitors.
4. **embossed:** covered with designs.

LIVING CHARACTERS

This story starts dramatically,
with Odysseus acting like an
action hero in the movies.

VOCABULARY

In line 11, I think *revelry* means
something like loud partying. And
throng must mean a crowd.

LIVING CHARACTERS

Homer makes even Antinous,
the leader of the suitors, whom
we haven't met before in these
selections, come alive. What
do you learn about him in
lines 8–13?

_____

_____

_____

_____

_____

_____

_____

_____

_____

Here's
HOW

VOCABULARY

I know that cranes are birds with long necks. So I think *craned* in line 21 means the suitors stretched their necks and strained to see.

Your
TURN

MONITOR YOUR COMPREHENSION

Read to the end of the page, and, on the lines below, retell in your own words what has happened since Odysseus killed Antinous. Then, predict what you think is going to happen next.

_____

_____

_____

_____

_____

_____

_____

_____

_____

_____

_____

_____

_____

_____

_____

_____

_____

_____

Backward and down he went, letting the wine cup fall

from his shocked hand. Like pipes his nostrils jetted

crimson runnels,[5] a river of mortal red,

and one last kick upset his table

20 knocking the bread and meat to soak in dusty blood.

Now as they craned to see their champion where he lay

the suitors jostled in uproar down the hall,

everyone on his feet. Wildly they turned and scanned

the walls in the long room for arms; but not a shield,

not a good ashen spear was there for a man to take and

25   throw.

IN OTHER WORDS Odysseus, dressed as a beggar, wins the archery contest. Then he throws off his rags and aims his bow and arrow at Antinous, the leader of the suitors. Antinous, who is drinking wine out of a golden cup, never sees the arrow. He falls dead, the arrow through his throat. The other suitors look around for their weapons.

All they could do was yell in outrage at Odysseus:

"Foul! to shoot at a man! That was your last shot!"

"Your own throat will be slit for this!"

"Our finest lad is down!

You killed the best on Ithaca."

"Buzzards will tear your eyes out!"

For they imagined as they wished—that it was a wild

30   shot,

an unintended killing—fools, not to comprehend

they were already in the grip of death.

_____

5. runnels: streams.

But glaring under his brows Odysseus answered:

"You yellow dogs, you thought I'd never make it
home from the land of Troy. You took my house to
35   plunder,
twisted my maids to serve your beds. You dared
bid for my wife while I was still alive.
Contempt[6] was all you had for the gods who rule wide
     heaven,
contempt for what men say of you hereafter.
40   Your last hour has come. You die in blood."

As they all took this in, sickly green fear
pulled at their entrails,[7] and their eyes flickered
looking for some hatch or hideaway from death.
Eurymachus[8] alone could speak. He said:

45   "If you are Odysseus of Ithaca come back,
all that you say these men have done is true.
Rash actions, many here, more in the countryside.
But here he lies, the man who caused them all.
Antinous was the ringleader, he whipped us on
50   to do these things. He cared less for a marriage
than for the power Cronion[9] has denied him
as king of Ithaca. For that
he tried to trap your son and would have killed him.

IN OTHER WORDS   The other suitors, weaponless,
shout threats at Odysseus. He answers that they have defied
the gods by coming into his house uninvited and wooing his
wife while he was still alive. Now they will die. At last, the
suitors realize who he is. Now filled with fear, they look for
an escape. Then Eurymachus speaks up. He admits that

---

6. **Contempt:** scorn.
7. **entrails:** guts.
8. **Eurymachus** (yoo RIHM uh kuhs): one of Penelope's suitors.
9. **Cronion:** another name for Zeus, meaning "son of Cronus."

Your TURN

VOCABULARY

Line 33 says Odysseus was *glaring*. What kind of look do you think he had on his face?

_____

_____

Here's HOW

MONITOR YOUR COMPREHENSION

The reasons Odysseus gives for killing all the suitors (lines 34–40) would probably get him jail for life, or maybe even the death penalty, in the United States today. But I read that epic heroes are supposed to represent the values of their society. That's why I think the ancient Greeks must have considered these very good reasons.

Your TURN

LIVING CHARACTERS

Eurymachus blames Antinous for all the bad things he and the other men have done (lines 45–53). What does that tell you about Eurymachus? Is it a cowardly or wise thing to say under the circumstances?

_____

_____

_____

_____

_____

what Odysseus says is true. He also points out that Antinous was the leader of the group, and he is dead.

He is dead now and has his portion. Spare
55 your own people. As for ourselves, we'll make
restitution of wine and meat consumed,
and add, each one, a tithe of twenty oxen
with gifts of bronze and gold to warm your heart.
Meanwhile we cannot blame you for your anger."

60 Odysseus glowered under his black brows
and said:

"Not for the whole treasure of your fathers,
all you enjoy, lands, flocks, or any gold
put up by others, would I hold my hand.
There will be killing till the score is paid.
You forced yourselves upon this house. Fight your
65   way out,
or run for it, if you think you'll escape death.
I doubt one man of you skins by." . . .

YOU NEED TO KNOW   Eurymachus begs Odysseus to spare the other suitors. They will pay him back for everything they took and more. Odysseus says no amount of treasure would make him spare their lives. Now, Odysseus' son, Telemachus, along with the swineherd and cowherd, join in the fight. The suitors are trapped, and many of them already lie dying on the floor.

At this moment that unmanning[10] thundercloud,
the aegis,[11] Athena's shield,
took form aloft in the great hall.

---

10. **unmanning:** terrifying.
11. **aegis** (EE juhs).

70 　　　　　　　　　And the suitors mad with fear
at her great sign stampeded like stung cattle by a river
when the dread shimmering gadfly strikes in summer,
in the flowering season, in the long-drawn days.
After them the attackers wheeled, as terrible as falcons
from eyries[12] in the mountains veering over and diving
75 　　　down
with talons wide unsheathed on flights of birds,

who cower down the sky in chutes[13] and bursts along the
　　　valley—
but the pouncing falcons grip their prey, no frantic wing
　　　avails,
and farmers love to watch those beakèd hunters.
80 So these now fell upon the suitors in that hall,
turning, turning to strike and strike again,
while torn men moaned at death, and blood ran smoking
over the whole floor. . . .

　　　　　　　　　　　　　　　(*from* Book 22)

IN OTHER WORDS　　The sign of Athena's shield
appears in the air over their heads. This supernatural symbol
of power terrorizes the suitors. They run like scared cattle,
but they can't escape. Odysseus, Telemachus, and their two
friends show the suitors no mercy. The suitors are
slaughtered in the great hall.

MONITOR YOUR COMPREHENSION

In lines 70–73, Homer uses a simile—a comparison using *like* or *as*—to describe how the suitors behave. And in lines 74–79, he uses another, longer simile to describe how Odysseus, Telemachus, and their two friends attack the suitors. Read each simile carefully, and try to visualize, or picture, the scene. Then, tell how each simile makes you feel about the scene described.

Lines 70–73: _____

_____

_____

_____

_____

_____

_____

_____

Lines 74–79: _____

_____

_____

_____

_____

_____

_____

_____

_____

12. **eyries** (EHR eez): nests built in high places.
13. **chutes:** waterfalls or river rapids.

Odysseus and Penelope

YOU NEED TO KNOW The nurse Eurycleia[1] runs to Penelope to announce the return of Odysseus and the defeat of the suitors. The faithful Penelope—the perfect wife for the clever Odysseus—suspects a trick from the gods and decides to test this stranger who claims to be her husband.

Crossing the doorsill she sat down at once
in firelight, against the nearest wall,
across the room from the lord Odysseus.
                                        There
leaning against a pillar, sat the man
5 and never lifted up his eyes, but only waited
for what his wife would say when she had seen him.
And she, for a long time, sat deathly still
in wonderment—for sometimes as she gazed
she found him—yes, clearly—like her husband,
10 but sometimes blood and rags were all she saw.
Telemachus's voice came to her ears:
                                        "Mother,
cruel mother, do you feel nothing,
drawing yourself apart this way from Father?
Will you not sit with him and talk and question him?
15 What other woman could remain so cold?
Who shuns her lord, and he come back to her
from wars and wandering, after twenty years?
Your heart is hard as flint and never changes!"

IN OTHER WORDS Penelope sits across the room from Odysseus and watches him, trying to recognize him under the blood and rags. Telemachus accuses his mother of being cruel and coldhearted. Her husband has returned after twenty years, and she ignores him. Why doesn't she speak to him?

---

1. **Eurycleia** (yoo rih KLY yuh): the old woman who took care of Odysseus when he was a baby.

Penelope answered:

"I am stunned, child.

20 I cannot speak to him. I cannot question him.
I cannot keep my eyes upon his face.
If really he is Odysseus, truly home,
beyond all doubt we two shall know each other
better than you or anyone. There are
secret signs we know, we two."

25   A smile
came now to the lips of the patient hero, Odysseus,
who turned to Telemachus and said:

"Peace: let your mother test me at her leisure.
Before long she will see and know me best.
30 These tatters, dirt—all that I'm caked with now—
make her look hard at me and doubt me still. . . ."

IN OTHER WORDS   Penelope tells her son that if this
man is really Odysseus, they will know each other by secret
signs. Odysseus smiles and agrees.

Greathearted Odysseus, home at last,
was being bathed now by Eurynome[2]
and rubbed with golden oil, and clothed again
35 in a fresh tunic and a cloak. Athena
lent him beauty, head to foot. She made him
taller, and massive, too, with crisping hair
in curls like petals of wild hyacinth[3]
but all red-golden. Think of gold infused[4]
40 on silver by a craftsman, whose fine art
Hephaestus[5] taught him, or Athena: one
whose work moves to delight: just so she lavished

---

2. **Eurynome** (yoo RIHN uh mee): Penelope's housekeeper.
3. **hyacinth:** a plant of the lily family, with sweet-smelling, bell-shaped petals.
4. **infused:** put into.
5. **Hephaestus** (hee FEHS tuhs): god of metalworking.

Your TURN

LIVING CHARACTERS

Circle in lines 26 and 32 the words Homer uses to describe Odysseus. Then, retell in your own words how Athena makes him look (lines 36–43).

_____
_____
_____
_____
_____
_____
_____
_____
_____
_____

Here's HOW

VOCABULARY

I've heard the phrase "lavished with praise." So I know _lavished_ in line 42 means "gave generously."

Your
TURN

VOCABULARY

Based on how Penelope is acting toward Odysseus, what do you think *aloof* means in line 48? Write your definition on the line below. Then, check your answer in a dictionary to see if you're right.

_____

_____

Your
TURN

LIVING CHARACTERS

Odysseus was described as patient (line 26) and greathearted (line 32). How, then, do you explain his complaint in lines 45–50? Write your answer on the lines below.

_____

_____

_____

_____

_____

_____

Here's
HOW

LIVING CHARACTERS

Odysseus and Penelope have both asked the nurse to make up a separate bed for Odysseus. I think they are just having a spat and acting mean when they really want to be friendly.

beauty over Odysseus' head and shoulders.
He sat then in the same chair by the pillar,
facing his silent wife, and said:

45   "Strange woman,
the immortals of Olympus made you hard,
harder than any. Who else in the world
would keep aloof as you do from her husband
if he returned to her from years of trouble,

50 cast on his own land in the twentieth year?

Nurse, make up a bed for me to sleep on.
Her heart is iron in her breast."

                               Penelope
spoke to Odysseus now. She said:

                           "Strange man,
if man you are . . . This is no pride on my part

55 nor scorn for you—not even wonder, merely.
I know so well how you—how he—appeared
boarding the ship for Troy. But all the same . . .

Make up his bed for him, Eurycleia.
Place it outside the bedchamber my lord

60 built with his own hands. Pile the big bed
with fleeces, rugs, and sheets of purest linen."

IN OTHER WORDS   Odysseus bathes and puts on fresh clothing. The goddess Athena helps, making Odysseus tall and handsome. Then he goes to Penelope and, like Telemachus, accuses her of a cold heart. Penelope asks the nurse to make up his own bed for him and to place it outside their bedroom.

With this she tried him to the breaking point,
and he turned on her in a flash, raging:
"Woman, by heaven you've stung me now!

65 Who dared to move my bed?
No builder had the skill for that—unless

a god came down to turn the trick. No mortal
in his best days could budge it with a crowbar.
There is our pact and pledge, our secret sign,
70   built into that bed—my handiwork
and no one else's!

                                An old trunk of olive
grew like a pillar on the building plot,
and I laid out our bedroom round that tree,
lined up the stone walls, built the walls and roof,
75   gave it a doorway and smooth-fitting doors.
Then I lopped off the silvery leaves and branches,
hewed and shaped the stump from the roots up
into a bedpost, drilled it, let it serve
as model for the rest, I planed them all,
80   inlaid them all with silver, gold, and ivory,
and stretched a bed between—a pliant[6] web
of oxhide thongs dyed crimson.

                            There's our sign!
I know no more. Could someone else's hand
have sawn that trunk and dragged the frame away?"

IN OTHER WORDS   Odysseus becomes very angry.
Who could have moved his bed? An olive tree grew on that
spot, and he had built their bed using the tree as a bedpost.
It was their secret sign. Had someone removed that tree and
taken his bed away?

85   Their secret! as she heard it told, her knees
grew tremulous[7] and weak, her heart failed her.
With eyes brimming tears she ran to him,
throwing her arms around his neck, and kissed him,
                                murmuring:
"Do not rage at me, Odysseus!
90   No one ever matched your caution! Think
what difficulty the gods gave: they denied us

---

6. **pliant:** flexible.
7. **tremulous:** trembling; shaking.

Your
TURN

MONITOR YOUR COMPREHENSION

Re-read lines 71–82. Then, describe in your own words the bed Odysseus made himself.

_____

_____

_____

_____

_____

_____

_____

_____

_____

Here's
HOW

VOCABULARY

I know that a plane is a woodworking tool. I think *planed* must mean "smoothed" in line 79.

MONITOR YOUR COMPREHENSION

I'll review what has just happened. Penelope tells Odysseus not to be mad at her and explains that she couldn't trust anyone all those years he was gone. She finally knows he is really Odysseus because he knows the secret of their bed.

Your
TURN

MONITOR YOUR COMPREHENSION

Do you think this tearful, loving reunion is a fitting ending for a heroic adventure story? Explain why or why not on the lines below.

_____
_____
_____
_____
_____
_____
_____
_____
_____
_____
_____
_____
_____
_____

life together in our prime and flowering years,

kept us from crossing into age together.

Forgive me, don't be angry. I could not

95 welcome you with love on sight! I armed myself

long ago against the frauds of men,

impostors[8] who might come—and all those many

whose underhanded ways bring evil on! . . .

But here and now, what sign could be so clear

100 as this of our own bed?

No other man has ever laid eyes on it—

only my own slave, Actoris, that my father

sent with me as a gift—she kept our door.

You make my stiff heart know that I am yours."

105 Now from his breast into his eyes the ache

of longing mounted, and he wept at last,

his dear wife, clear and faithful, in his arms,

longed for

    as the sun-warmed earth is longed for by a swimmer

spent in rough water where his ship went down

110 under Poseidon's blows, gale winds and tons of sea.

Few men can keep alive through a big surf

to crawl, clotted[9] with brine,[10] on kindly beaches

in joy, in joy, knowing the abyss[11] behind:

and so she too rejoiced, her gaze upon her husband,

115 her white arms round him pressed, as though forever. . . .

(*from* Book 23)

IN OTHER WORDS Now Penelope knows that this man is really Odysseus. She bursts into tears and runs to kiss him, asking him to forgive her—she had to be sure. They embrace and weep.

---

8. **impostors:** people who pretend to be someone other than themselves.
9. **clotted:** here, covered or caked.
10. **brine:** very salty water.
11. **abyss:** a bottomless gulf or pit.

Living Characters

You get to know what characters in literature are like the same way you get to know real people: from what they say and do, what others say about them, and how they are described. In the chart below, fill in an example of what you learn about Odysseus, Telemachus, and Penelope by each of these methods. Some have been done for you.

	Odysseus	Telemachus	Penelope
1. What they say	"Your last hour is come. You die in blood."		
2. What they do		He is polite and thoughtful when he offers an old beggar a seat.	
3. What other characters say about them			The swineherd says, "Her nights and days are wearied out with grieving."
4. How they are described by the narrator	The narrator describes him as noble and enduring.		

Heroes with Solid Feet

Reading Skill: Evaluating an Author's Argument

How would you persuade your parents to let you go to a party? First, you'd probably think about the **intent,** or purpose, of your argument. Then, you'd need to give your parents reasons that support your argument. A **logical appeal** would present facts and statistics, and an **emotional appeal** would probably present your needs and wishes. You might also want to consider the **tone** of your argument. Would you be serious, argumentative, or even humorous? These same elements are a part of every argument. Identifying these elements in an essay can help you evaluate an author's argument.

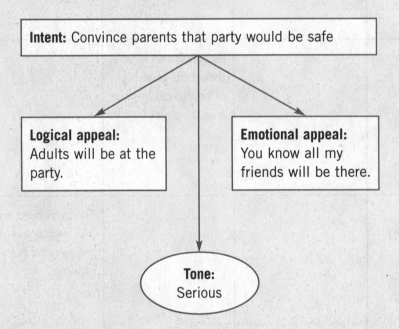

Intent: Convince parents that party would be safe

Logical appeal: Adults will be at the party.

Emotional appeal: You know all my friends will be there.

Tone: Serious

Into the Essay

Berlin was the German capital during the rule of Adolf Hitler and the Nazi Party. By the end of World War II, more than six million European Jews had died in German concentration camps. Some Germans, however, helped their Jewish friends and neighbors. The author of "Heroes with Solid Feet," Kirk Douglas, is a Hollywood star who was born in 1916.

Heroes with Solid Feet

BASED ON THE ESSAY BY
Kirk Douglas

Recently I traveled to Berlin to accept a lifetime achievement award from the Berlin Film Festival. I smiled at the idea that this award supposedly marked the end of what I will achieve in my life.

I accepted the award because I was curious to see Berlin again.
5 During my earlier visits there, a wall that separated Communist East Berlin and democratic West Berlin had divided the city.

When I met with journalists, one of them asked, "As a Jew, how does it affect you to be in Berlin?" The pictures we have all seen raced through my mind. I saw shattering glass windows, Hitler salutes, Jews
10 being herded into freight cars. I saw piles of emaciated Jews dying of starvation, and I saw ovens with dark smoke coming out of chimneys.

I said that the last hundred years had been terrible because there had been so many wars. In Germany the Holocaust, the attempt to destroy the Jews as a people, was perhaps the worst crime of all. I
15 went on to say, "But I don't think children should be punished for the sins of their fathers."

The questioner asked again, "So why did you come back to Berlin?" The question bothered me because, after all that had happened, I didn't know a good reason for a Jew to be in Berlin.
20 That night my wife and I had dinner with friends and a Jewish friend of theirs who had lived in Berlin during the war. She was a happy person, even though her parents and grandparents had been killed in German camps. I asked her, "So, why do you stay in Berlin?"

Smiling, she answered, "I owe that to the little heroes." She told
25 me about all the Germans who had hidden her during the war. She said she had been lucky to find little heroes who helped her survive. "Not everyone here was wicked," she said.

Her story had a big effect on me. We look for big heroes as role models, but often we find out that the people we try to copy have feet
30 of clay, or flaws. When they topple, we realize they were not heroes after all. It's better to look for little heroes, and to try to be one. You don't have to save a life—you only need to try to help other people.

If everyone tried, just think of the lifetime achievements we'd all have.

Evaluating an Argument

Intent and Tone

Use the chart below to evaluate the argument in "Heroes with Solid Feet." First, think about the author's **intent,** and describe it in the first box. Then, identify the support for the author's argument as logical or emotional. Put a check mark in the box next to your answer, and list the support the author uses. Finally, describe the **tone** of the argument in the last box. One box is filled in for you.

Author's Intent

Persuade readers that real heroes are ordinary people who try to help other people.

Support for Argument

Logical appeal ☐   Emotional appeal ☐

Author's Tone

From The Tragedy of Romeo and Juliet
Act II, Scene 2

Literary Focus: Tragedy and Figures of Speech

A **tragedy** is a narrative—usually a play—about serious and important actions that ends unhappily. Most often a tragedy ends in the death of one or more of the main characters. Sometimes the disaster happens to an innocent character, but often the character has some flaw that leads to his or her downfall.

Figures of speech are comparisons between unlike things. **Similes** are comparisons using *like* or *as: I ran like a cheetah toward the finish line*. **Metaphors** are comparisons that say one thing *is* another thing: *I was a cheetah running toward the finish line*. **Personification** gives human qualities to something that is not human: *The silvery moon smiled through the clouds.*

Reading Skill: Connecting with the Text

Many of the emotions and conflicts in this four-hundred-year-old play are ones we experience today. When you **connect with the text,** you make links between what is happening in the text and your own world. As you read, think about how the events in the text relate to your own life or to events you have read about.

Into the Play

In William Shakespeare's *The Tragedy of Romeo and Juliet,* a young man and a nearly fourteen-year-old girl fall in love at first sight. But their families are enemies, so Romeo and Juliet hide their love, which leads to tragedy.

The Tragedy of Romeo and Juliet

Act II, Scene 2

William Shakespeare

Act II, Scene 2

YOU NEED TO KNOW Romeo Montague and Juliet Capulet have just met at a party at her parents' house. They fell in love at first sight, but their families are sworn enemies. Now Romeo waits outside in the darkness, hoping for a glimpse of Juliet.

Shakespeare wrote this play over four hundred years ago. Of course, the English language has changed a lot since then. Here are some guidelines to understanding Shakespeare's English:

- Some verbs have different endings from today's versions, such as *doth* for *does* and *art* for *are*
- *Thou* and *thee* mean *you*, and *thy* means *your*
- *Wherefore* means *why*

As you read the play, look for more vocabulary clues in the footnotes and sidewrap.

Scene 2. *Capulet's Orchard*

Romeo *(coming forward).*

He jests at scars that never felt a wound.

[*Enter* JULIET *at a window.*]

But soft! What light through yonder window breaks?
It is the East, and Juliet is the sun!
Arise, fair sun, and kill the envious moon,
5   Who is already sick and pale with grief
That thou her maid[1] art far more fair than she.
Be not her maid, since she is envious.
Her vestal livery[2] is but sick and green,[3]
And none but fools do wear it. Cast it off.
10 It is my lady! O, it is my love!
O, that she knew she were!

___

1. **thou her maid:** Romeo is speaking of Juliet, whom he sees as servant of the goddess of the moon, Diana.
2. **vestal livery:** clothing of a maiden.
3. **sick and green:** Unmarried girls supposedly had "greensickness," or anemia. Anemia is a condition in which a person's blood has too little iron, which can cause the skin to have a greenish color.

VOCABULARY

I'm not sure what the word *jests* means in line 1. I know from history that a court jester was someone hired by kings and queens to make people laugh. I bet *jests* means "makes fun of."

FIGURES OF SPEECH

I can see in lines 2–9 that Romeo is using a metaphor to directly compare Juliet to the sun. He goes on to personify the moon. He says the moon is jealous of the beautiful sun (Juliet).

She speaks, yet she says nothing. What of that?

Her eye discourses;[4] I will answer it.

I am too bold; 'tis not to me she speaks.

15   Two of the fairest stars in all the heaven,

Having some business, do entreat her eyes

To twinkle in their spheres till they return.

What if her eyes were there, they in her head?

The brightness of her cheek would shame those stars

20   As daylight doth a lamp; her eyes in heaven

Would through the airy region stream so bright

That birds would sing and think it were not night.

See how she leans her cheek upon her hand!

O, that I were a glove upon that hand,

25   That I might touch that cheek!

IN OTHER WORDS   Juliet appears at her window. Romeo, seeing her, makes a long speech to himself about her beauty. He compares her to the rising sun; he says she is more beautiful than the moon. He says her eyes are like stars. Romeo clearly has a crush on this girl whom he has just met.

Juliet.   Ay me!

Romeo.   She speaks.

O, speak again, bright angel, for thou art

As glorious to this night, being o'er my head,

As is a wingèd messenger of heaven

Unto the white-upturnèd wond'ring eyes

30   Of mortals that fall back to gaze on him

When he bestrides[5] the lazy puffing clouds

And sails upon the bosom of the air.

Juliet.

O Romeo, Romeo! Wherefore art thou Romeo?[6]

Deny thy father and refuse thy name;

---

4. **discourses:** speaks.
5. **bestrides:** rides straddled as if riding a horse.
6. In other words, "Why is your name Romeo?" (It is the name of her enemy.)

FIGURES OF SPEECH

I had to read lines 15–21 several times to see the metaphor. Romeo is saying that Juliet's cheeks and eyes are so bright that they put the stars to shame.

VOCABULARY

My teacher told us that the little marks over some words, like "wingèd" in line 28, show how the word is pronounced: WEENG uhd. But it still means the same thing as *winged*, that is, "having wings."

FIGURES OF SPEECH

Romeo is gazing at Juliet standing above him on the balcony. In lines 26–32, he compares her to something. Circle the words that show what he compares her to.

Your TURN

CONNECTING WITH THE TEXT

Lines 38–49 are a soliloquy (suh LIHL uh kwee)—a speech in which the character is speaking to herself. In real life people would think these thoughts silently, but in a play the audience wouldn't then hear them! This is one way a play is different from real life. Re-read lines 52–61. Aside from the poetic language, do you think this is the way new lovers would react today? Explain your response on the lines below.

_____

_____

_____

_____

_____

_____

_____

_____

35　Or, if thou wilt not, be but sworn my love,

　　And I'll no longer be a Capulet.

Romeo (aside).

　　Shall I hear more, or shall I speak at this?

Juliet.

　　'Tis but thy name that is my enemy.

　　Thou art thyself, though not[7] a Montague.

40　What's Montague? It is nor hand, nor foot,

　　Nor arm, nor face. O, be some other name

　　Belonging to a man.

　　What's in a name? That which we call a rose

　　By any other word would smell as sweet.

45　So Romeo would, were he not Romeo called,

　　Retain that dear perfection which he owes[8]

　　Without that title. Romeo, doff[9] thy name;

　　And for thy name, which is no part of thee,

　　Take all myself.

Romeo.　　　　　　　I take thee at thy word.

50　Call me but love, and I'll be new baptized;

　　Henceforth I never will be Romeo.

Juliet.

　　What man art thou, that, thus bescreened[10] in night,

　　So stumblest on my counsel?[11]

Romeo.　　　　　　　　　By a name

　　I know not how to tell thee who I am.

55　My name, dear saint, is hateful to myself

　　Because it is an enemy to thee.

　　Had I it written, I would tear the word.

Juliet.

　　My ears have yet not drunk a hundred words

　　Of thy tongue's uttering, yet I know the sound.

60　Art thou not Romeo, and a Montague?

---

7. **though not:** even if you were not.
8. **owes:** owns.
9. **doff:** put aside.
10. **bescreened:** hidden away.
11. **counsel:** private thoughts.

Romeo.

    Neither, fair maid, if either thee dislike.

IN OTHER WORDS   Juliet, not knowing Romeo is listening below, talks to herself about him. Why must he be a Montague, an enemy of her family? She compares Romeo to a rose, which would smell just as nice even if it had some other name than "rose." Why couldn't he be the same person, but with a different name? Romeo speaks up, saying that he would gladly change his name for her sake. Juliet is frightened—who has overheard her? Romeo answers that he cannot tell her his name because she hates it and therefore so does he. Juliet recognizes his voice.

Juliet.

    How camest thou hither, tell me, and wherefore?

    The orchard walls are high and hard to climb,

    And the place death, considering who thou art,

65   If any of my kinsmen find thee here.

Romeo.

    With love's light wings did I o'erperch[12] these walls;

    For stony limits cannot hold love out,

    And what love can do, that dares love attempt.

    Therefore thy kinsmen are no stop to me.

Juliet.

70   If they do see thee, they will murder thee.

Romeo.

    Alack, there lies more peril in thine eye

    Than twenty of their swords! Look thou but sweet,

    And I am proof[13] against their enmity.

Juliet.

    I would not for the world they saw thee here.

Romeo.

75   I have night's cloak to hide me from their eyes;

---

12. **o'erperch:** fly over.
13. **proof:** armored.

Here's HOW

FIGURES OF SPEECH

In line 66, I see a metaphor—Romeo says he flew over the walls on wings of love. Romeo doesn't have wings, and neither does love. I think he means that his love makes him feel light and free like a bird.

Here's HOW

VOCABULARY

In lines 71 and 73, I see two words I don't understand: *peril* and *enmity.* Since Romeo compares peril to twenty swords in the next line, I think *peril* means "danger." *Enmity* is harder to figure out. It sounds kind of like *enemy,* but that word doesn't exactly fit here. My dictionary says *enmity* means "feelings of hatred against an enemy."

Here's HOW

TRAGEDY

I know that a tragedy ends unhappily. I wonder if all this talk about Juliet's relatives killing Romeo foreshadows, or hints at, what is to come. Romeo says her love will protect him from them, though, so maybe he will die some other way.

Your
TURN

FIGURES OF SPEECH

In lines 80–81, Romeo personifies love. Underline the human qualiities of love in these lines.

Your
TURN

CONNECTING WITH THE TEXT

In lines 85–106, Juliet is embarrassed that Romeo has overheard her words of love. Do you think a teenage girl of today would be just as embarrassed if the boy she loved overheard her gushing about him? Explain.

_____

_____

_____

_____

_____

_____

_____

_____

_____

_____

_____

_____

_____

And but[14] thou love me, let them find me here.

My life were better ended by their hate

Than death proroguèd,[15] wanting of thy love.

Juliet.

By whose direction found'st thou out this place?

Romeo.

80 By Love, that first did prompt me to inquire.

He lent me counsel, and I lent him eyes.

I am no pilot; yet, wert thou as far

As that vast shore washed with the farthest sea,

I should adventure for such merchandise.

IN OTHER WORDS Juliet wonders how Romeo got onto her family's property. She warns him that he will be killed if he is discovered there. Romeo is not afraid; all he cares about is Juliet. He says he would rather die than live without her love. When she asks how he found her garden, Romeo tells her that Love guided him there.

Juliet.

85 Thou knowest the mask of night is on my face;

Else would a maiden blush bepaint my cheek

For that which thou hast heard me speak tonight.

Fain[16] would I dwell on form—fain, fain deny

What I have spoke; but farewell compliment.[17]

90 Dost thou love me? I know thou wilt say "Ay";

And I will take thy word. Yet, if thou swear'st,

Thou mayst prove false. At lovers' perjuries,[18]

They say Jove[19] laughs. O gentle Romeo,

If thou dost love, pronounce it faithfully.

95 Or if thou think'st I am too quickly won,

I'll frown and be perverse[20] and say thee nay,

---

14. **but:** if only.
15. **proroguèd:** postponed.
16. **Fain:** gladly.
17. **compliment:** good manners.
18. **perjuries:** broken promises.
19. **Jove:** Roman god.
20. **perverse:** contrary or stubborn; that is, Juliet will act like she doesn't like Romeo.

So thou wilt woo; but else, not for the world.

In truth, fair Montague, I am too fond,[21]

And therefore thou mayst think my havior[22] light;

100 But trust me, gentleman, I'll prove more true

Than those that have more cunning to be strange.[23]

I should have been more strange, I must confess,

But that thou overheard'st, ere I was ware,

My true love passion. Therefore pardon me,

105 And not impute[24] this yielding to light love,

Which the dark night hath so discoverèd.[25]

Romeo.

Lady, by yonder blessèd moon I vow,

That tips with silver all these fruit-tree tops—

Juliet.

O, swear not by the moon, the inconstant moon,

110 That monthly changes in her circle orb,

Lest that thy love prove likewise variable.

Romeo.

What shall I swear by?

Juliet.   Do not swear at all;

Or if thou wilt, swear by thy gracious self,

Which is the god of my idolatry,

115 And I'll believe thee.

Romeo.   If my heart's dear love—

Juliet.

Well, do not swear. Although I joy in thee,

I have no joy of this contract tonight.

It is too rash, too unadvised, too sudden;

Too like the lightning, which doth cease to be

120 Ere one can say it lightens. Sweet, good night!

This bud of love, by summer's ripening breath,

May prove a beauteous flower when next we meet.

Good night, good night! As sweet repose and rest

Come to thy heart as that within my breast!

---

21. **fond:** affectionate, tender.
22. **havior:** behavior.
23. **strange:** aloof or cold.
24. **impute:** falsely blame.
25. **discoverèd:** revealed.

THE TRAGEDY OF ROMEO AND JULIET, ACT II, SCENE 2 **155**

Here's
HOW

VOCABULARY

I'm not sure what the word *cunning* in line 101 means, but I think it means "craftiness." I checked a dictionary, and I was right.

Your
TURN

FIGURES OF SPEECH

The word *idolatry* in line 114 means "worship of an idol or idols." An *idol* is an object that represents a god. Who is the "god" Juliet is referring to?

_____

_____

Your
TURN

VOCABULARY

The word *rash* can mean "an eruption of red spots on the skin" or "hasty." Which meaning fits line 118?

_____

_____

Romeo.

125   O, wilt thou leave me so unsatisfied?

IN OTHER WORDS   Juliet is embarrassed that Romeo heard her private thoughts. But since it is too late to pretend she doesn't care for him, she asks if he loves her. Juliet is afraid that Romeo will not take her love seriously and think it is given too easily. Romeo eagerly begins to swear his love by the moon. Juliet stops him, saying she hopes his love will not be as changeable as the moon. In fact, she doesn't want him to swear his love at all. It's all happening too fast for her. She wants them to take more time, let their love grow. But Romeo is not ready to say good night.

Juliet.

        What satisfaction canst thou have tonight?

Romeo.

        The exchange of thy love's faithful vow for mine.

Juliet.

        I gave thee mine before thou didst request it;

        And yet I would it were to give again.

Romeo.

130   Wouldst thou withdraw it? For what purpose, love?

Juliet.

        But to be frank[26] and give it thee again.

        And yet I wish but for the thing I have.

        My bounty[27] is as boundless as the sea,

        My love as deep; the more I give to thee,

135   The more I have, for both are infinite.

        I hear some noise within. Dear love, adieu!

[NURSE *calls within.*]

        Anon,[28] good nurse! Sweet Montague, be true.

        Stay but a little, I will come again.   [*Exit.*]

---

26. **frank:** generous.
27. **bounty:** ability to give.
28. **Anon:** soon.

Your TURN

FIGURES OF SPEECH

Circle the figure of speech in line 133. Is it a simile or a metaphor? Explain how you know.

Romeo.

> O blessèd, blessèd night! I am afeard,
140 > Being in night, all this is but a dream,
> Too flattering-sweet to be substantial.

[*Enter* JULIET *again.*]

Juliet.

> Three words, dear Romeo, and good night indeed.
> If that thy bent[29] of love be honorable,
> Thy purpose marriage, send me word tomorrow,
145 > By one that I'll procure[30] to come to thee,
> Where and what time thou wilt perform the rite;
> And all my fortunes at thy foot I'll lay
> And follow thee my lord throughout the world.

Nurse (*within*). Madam!

Juliet.

150 > I come anon.—But if thou meanest not well,
> I do beseech[31] thee—

IN OTHER WORDS   Romeo wants them both to swear their love. Juliet says she already has; her love for him is endless. She hears her nurse calling, and she disappears inside. Romeo asks himself if he is dreaming. Juliet reappears. She says if he really loves her, he must send her a message tomorrow, giving a time and place for their wedding, and she will come. She will send someone to get Romeo's message.

Nurse (*within*). Madam!

Juliet.   By and by I come.—

> To cease thy strife[32] and leave me to my grief.
> Tomorrow will I send.

---

29. **bent:** intention.
30. **procure:** get.
31. **beseech:** beg.
32. **strife:** efforts to win her.

VOCABULARY

The word *substantial* in line 141 means either "real" or "large." Which meaning fits this line best?

CONNECTING WITH THE TEXT

Even though this play was written a long time ago, I know a lot of kids today are in this kind of rush, too. When I read lines 142–148, I can tell Juliet is definitely a teenager. She's only known Romeo a few hours, and already she wants to marry him and follow him all over the world.

VOCABULARY

I think I know what "hist" means in line 159. Since Juliet has just come back, she's trying to get Romeo's attention.

FIGURES OF SPEECH

In lines 168–170, Juliet plans to send a messenger to Romeo. Why do you think Juliet says waiting until the next morning will take "twenty years"?

_____

_____

_____

_____

Your TURN

CONNECTING WITH THE TEXT

Did you ever do something and then forget why you just did it? Why do you think Juliet forgets the reason she called Romeo back (line 171)?

_____

_____

_____

_____

_____

_____

Romeo.   So thrive my soul—

155 **Juliet.**

A thousand times good night!   [*Exit.*]

Romeo.

A thousand times the worse, to want thy light!

Love goes toward love as schoolboys from their books;

But love from love, toward school with heavy looks.

[*Enter* JULIET *again.*]

Juliet.

Hist! Romeo, hist! O for a falc'ner's voice

160 To lure this tassel gentle³³ back again!

Bondage is hoarse³⁴ and may not speak aloud,

Else would I tear the cave where Echo³⁵ lies

And make her airy tongue more hoarse than mine

With repetition of "My Romeo!"

165 **Romeo.**

It is my soul that calls upon my name.

How silver-sweet sound lovers' tongues by night,

Like softest music to attending ears!

Juliet.

Romeo!

Romeo.

          My sweet?

Juliet.   What o'clock tomorrow

Shall I send to thee?

Romeo.   By the hour of nine.

170 **Juliet.**

I will not fail. 'Tis twenty years till then.

I have forgot why I did call thee back.

Romeo.

Let me stand here till thou remember it.

Juliet.

I shall forget, to have thee still stand there,

---

33. **tassel gentle:** male falcon.
34. **Bondage is hoarse:** Juliet is in "bondage" to her parents and must whisper.
35. **Echo:** girl in a myth who could only repeat others' final words.

Rememb'ring how I love thy company.

175 **Romeo.**

And I'll still stay, to have thee still forget,

Forgetting any other home but this.

Juliet.

'Tis almost morning. I would have thee gone—

And yet no farther than a wanton's[36] bird,

180   That lets it hop a little from his hand,

Like a poor prisoner in his twisted gyves,[37]

And with a silken thread plucks it back again,

So loving-jealous of his liberty.

Romeo.

I would I were thy bird.

Juliet.   Sweet, so would I.

185   Yet I should kill thee with much cherishing.

Good night, good night! Parting is such sweet sorrow

That I shall say good night till it be morrow.   [*Exit.*]

Romeo.

Sleep dwell upon thine eyes, peace in thy breast!

Would I were sleep and peace, so sweet to rest!

190   Hence will I to my ghostly friar's[38] close cell,[39]

His help to crave and my dear hap[40] to tell.   [*Exit.*]

IN OTHER WORDS   Juliet's nurse calls again, and
they say good night. Romeo is sad to see her go. Juliet comes
out again, and they whisper more words of love back and
forth. He tells her to send her messenger by 9:00 A.M., and
she agrees. They linger, eager for any excuse not to leave
each other. Juliet wants him safely away before morning, but
she cannot stand to let him go. At last, she goes inside.
Romeo heads off to see the friar and ask if he will marry them
tomorrow.

---

36. wanton's: spoiled child's.
37. gyves (jyvz): chains, like the threads that hold the bird captive.
38. ghostly friar's: spiritual father's.
39. cell: small monastery.
40. hap: luck.

Here's HOW

FIGURES OF SPEECH

Juliet uses a metaphor in
lines 177–182 to compare Romeo
to a pet bird on a string. I think
she means that she wishes she
could pull Romeo back to her
side whenever she wants him.

Your TURN

CONNECTING WITH THE TEXT

In line 185 is one of
Shakespeare's many phrases
that people have loved and
quoted for hundreds of years:
"Parting is such sweet sorrow."
What do you think makes this
phrase so popular even today?

_____
_____
_____
_____
_____
_____
_____
_____
_____

Figures of Speech

In *The Tragedy of Romeo and Juliet,* William Shakespeare uses many figures of speech—imaginative comparisons of unlike things. Shakespeare's figures of speech are fresh images that we remember long after reading them.

Below are some examples of figures of speech from Act II, Scene 2. Read each example in the left box, and then explain what it means in the right box. The first one has been done for you.

Figures of Speech	Meaning
1. "But soft! What light through yonder window breaks? / It is the East, and Juliet is the sun!" (lines 2–3)	Juliet's beauty is so bright that she is like the rising sun.
2. "This bud of love, by summer's ripening breath, / May prove a beauteous flower when next we meet." (lines 121–122)	
3. "My bounty is as boundless as the sea, / My love as deep; the more I give to thee, / The more I have, for both are infinite." (lines 133–135)	
4. "Love goes toward love as schoolboys from their books; / But love from love, toward school with heavy looks." (lines 157–158)	

Vocabulary Development

Developing Vocabulary

Carefully read each word's definition, explanation, and sample sentence. Then, write a sentence of your own using that word.

1. **perverse** (puhr VURS) *adj.:* stubborn, contrary.

   My perverse sister refused to loan me her sweater even though I let her borrow my gloves yesterday.

   • *Perverse* can also be used to mean "wrong" or "improper."

   My sentence: _____

   _____

   _____

2. **counsel** (KOWN suhl) *n.:* private thoughts, secret plan.

   Even in the face of threats, the man stubbornly kept his counsel.

   • This meaning of *counsel* is in the expression "to keep one's own counsel," meaning "to keep one's thoughts and plans to oneself."

   My sentence: _____

   _____

   _____

3. **bounty** (BOWN tee) *n.:* ability to give.

   Grandma Jones was much loved for her bounty at holiday time.

   • *Bounty* can also mean "a generous gift," as well as "a reward given by the government for raising certain crops, capturing criminals, etc."

   My sentence: _____

   _____

   _____

From The Tragedy of Romeo and Juliet
Act III, Scene 5

Literary Focus: Dramatic Irony

Dramatic irony occurs when the reader knows something important that a character in a play or story does not know. A familiar example of dramatic irony is Little Red Riding Hood knocking innocently on Grandma's front door. We know about the wolf in the bed wearing Grandma's bonnet, but Little Red is unaware of the toothy surprise that awaits her.

Reading Skill: Paraphrasing

Paraphrasing means restating text in your own words. When you paraphrase a text, it makes the text easier to understand. Follow this checklist when you paraphrase:

- Make sure you understand the main idea of the text.
- Look up unfamiliar words.
- Replace difficult words with simple ones.
- Restate figures of speech in your own words, making clear what's being compared to what.
- Include all the details from the original.

Into the Play

Do you suppose there was an actual Romeo and Juliet? According to the people of Verona, Italy, Romeo Montague and Juliet Capulet did exist—they lived and died in Verona seven hundred years ago. Their story of tragic love has been retold many times in other theater and film works. You may have heard of the musical *West Side Story.* In that retelling, the two lovers come from rival gangs and different ethnic backgrounds.

From

The Tragedy of Romeo and Juliet

Act III, Scene 5

William Shakespeare

My teacher said the word *pomegranate* in line 4 is pronounced "PAHM uh GRAN iht." He brought a pomegranate to class today. It is a round fruit covered with a tough red rind. When my teacher cut it in half, I saw that it has a lot of seeds covered by pulp. It's kind of weird-looking, to be honest. But I might buy one myself so I can taste it!

Here's
HOW

PARAPHRASING

I'll try to paraphrase Romeo's lines (6-11): It was a lark (a bird that sings in the early morning), not a nightingale (which sings at night). Look, sweetheart, at the sunlight shining through the clouds in the east. The stars are gone, and the daylight is shining on top of the mountains. I have to go if I want to live; if I stay, I'll die.

Act III, Scene 5

> **YOU NEED TO KNOW**   Romeo and Juliet have been secretly married by Friar Laurence. Unaware of this event, Juliet's father has promised Paris, a young man who is interested in Juliet, that she will marry him. The wedding date is set. Romeo has killed Tybalt (Juliet's cousin) in a duel and has been banished. He must leave Verona and never return. But first, Romeo and Juliet have spent their wedding night together. They must say their final farewell before Romeo leaves for Mantua.

Scene 5. *Capulet's orchard*

Enter ROMEO *and* JULIET *aloft.*

Juliet.

> Wilt thou be gone? It is not yet near day.
> It was the nightingale, and not the lark,
> That pierced the fearful hollow of thine ear.
> Nightly she sings on yond pomegranate tree.
> 5 Believe me, love, it was the nightingale.

Romeo.

> It was the lark, the herald[1] of the morn;
> No nightingale. Look, love, what envious streaks
> Do lace the severing clouds in yonder east.
> Night's candles are burnt out, and jocund[2] day
> 10 Stands tiptoe on the misty mountaintops.
> I must be gone and live, or stay and die.

Juliet.

> Yond light is not daylight; I know it, I.
> It is some meteor that the sun exhales[3]
> To be to thee this night a torchbearer
> 15 And light thee on thy way to Mantua.
> Therefore stay yet; thou need'st not to be gone.

---

1. **herald:** someone who announces an event before it happens.
2. **jocund:** merry.
3. **exhales:** gives off. (It was believed that the sun drew up vapors and lit them as meteors.)

Romeo.

Let me be taken, let me be put to death.

I am content, so thou wilt have it so.

I'll say yon gray is not the morning's eye,

20   'Tis but the pale reflex[4] of Cynthia's brow;[5]

Nor that is not the lark whose notes do beat

The vaulty heaven so high above our heads.

I have more care to stay than will to go.

Come, death, and welcome! Juliet wills it so.

25   How is't, my soul? Let's talk; it is not day.

Juliet.

It is, it is! Hie hence, be gone, away!

It is the lark that sings so out of tune,

Straining harsh discords and unpleasing sharps.[6]

Some say the lark makes sweet division;[7]

30   This doth not so, for she divideth us.

Some say the lark and loathèd toad change eyes;[8]

O, now I would they had changed voices too,

Since arm from arm that voice doth us affray,[9]

Hunting thee hence with hunt's-up[10] to the day.

35   O, now be gone! More light and light it grows.

Romeo.

More light and light—more dark and dark our woes.

IN OTHER WORDS   It is dawn, and Romeo must leave, or he will be put to death. But Juliet refuses to believe that morning is near. They hear a lark sing; she says it is a nightingale. Romeo points to the sun, and Juliet says it is a meteor. Romeo gives in and says he is willing to stay and face death if that is what she wants. Juliet quickly changes her mind and urges him to leave.

---

4. **reflex:** reflection.
5. **Cynthia's brow:** Cynthia is the moon.
6. **harsh discords … unpleasing sharps:** the lark's song is characterized by disharmony and out-of-tune notes.
7. **division:** literally, a rapid run of notes, but Juliet is punning on the word's other meaning · (separation).
8. A fable to explain why the lark, which sings so beautifully, has ugly eyes, and why the toad, which croaks so harshly, has beautiful ones.
9. **affray:** frighten.
10. **hunt's-up:** morning song for hunters.

Here's HOW

PARAPHRASING

Here is how I'd paraphrase lines 17–20: Let me be taken and put to death. I am happy if that's the way you want it. I'll say the gray up there is not the approaching morning—it's only the pale reflection of the moon.

Your TURN

PARAPHRASING

How would you paraphrase lines 35–36?

_____
_____
_____
_____
_____
_____
_____
_____
_____
_____
_____
_____
_____
_____
_____

[_Enter_ NURSE.]

Nurse. Madam!

Juliet. Nurse?

Nurse.

 Your lady mother is coming to your chamber.

40 The day is broke; be wary, look about.   [_Exit._]

Juliet.

 Then, window, let day in, and let life out.

Romeo.

 Farewell, farewell! One kiss, and I'll descend.

[_He goes down._]

Juliet.

 Art thou gone so, love-lord, ay husband-friend?

 I must hear from thee every day in the hour,

45 For in a minute there are many days.

 O, for this count I shall be much in years

 Ere I again behold my Romeo!

Romeo.

 Farewell!

 I will omit no opportunity

50 That may convey[11] my greetings, love, to thee.

Juliet.

 O, think'st thou we shall ever meet again?

Romeo.

 I doubt it not; and all these woes shall serve

 For sweet discourses in our times to come.

Juliet.

 O God, I have an ill-divining soul![12]

55 Methinks I see thee, now thou art so low,

 As one dead in the bottom of a tomb.

 Either my eyesight fails, or thou look'st pale.

Romeo.

 And trust me, love, in my eye so do you.

---

11. **convey:** send.
12. **ill-divining soul:** a soul that senses a terrible future.

Dry[13] sorrow drinks our blood. Adieu, adieu!   [*Exit.*]

Juliet.

60   O Fortune, Fortune! All men call thee fickle.

If thou art fickle, what dost thou with him

That is renowned for faith? Be fickle, Fortune,

For then I hope thou wilt not keep him long

But send him back.

IN OTHER WORDS   Juliet's nurse comes in to warn her that her mother is coming. Romeo kisses Juliet goodbye and climbs down from her window. Juliet sadly tells him that every minute they are apart will feel like days. Romeo promises to send messages whenever he can, and he also says he is certain they will be together again someday. Juliet looks down at Romeo from her window and imagines that she is seeing him dead in a tomb. Romeo tells her that sorrow has made them both look pale and then departs. Juliet wonders when Fortune will send Romeo back to her again.

[*Enter* JULIET's *mother,* LADY CAPULET.]

Lady Capulet.

65   Ho, daughter! Are you up?

Juliet.

Who is't that calls? It is my lady mother.

Is she not down so late,[14] or up so early?

What unaccustomed cause procures her hither?[15]

Lady Capulet.

Why, how now, Juliet?

Juliet.   Madam, I am not well.

Lady Capulet.

70   Evermore weeping for your cousin's death?

What, wilt thou wash him from his grave with tears?

And if thou couldst, thou couldst not make him live.

Here's HOW

VOCABULARY

I am not sure what *fickle* means in line 60. Juliet speaks of Fortune keeping Romeo but then sending him back, making Fortune seem like it can't make up its mind. I think *fickle* means "changeable"— a changeable person can't commit to anything.

Your TURN

DRAMATIC IRONY

In line 70, Lady Capulet assumes that Juliet is weeping for her cousin Tybalt's death. What do we know that Juliet's mother does not know?

_____

_____

_____

_____

_____

_____

_____

_____

_____

_____

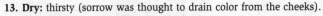

13. **Dry:** thirsty (sorrow was thought to drain color from the cheeks).
14. **down so late:** so late getting to bed.
15. **What unaccustomed . . . her hither?:** What on earth could bring her here?

VOCABULARY

The word *want* can mean "desire" or "lack." Which meaning is correct in line 74?

DRAMATIC IRONY

Nearly all of Juliet's responses to her parents have double meanings. Re-read lines 70–80 very closely to notice how Juliet can say one thing while her mother thinks she means something else. This is dramatic irony, since you know what Juliet really means but her mother doesn't. Who is Juliet really talking about?

PARAPHRASING

This is how I would paraphrase Lady Capulet's words in lines 79-80: Well, girl, you're not weeping for his death as much as you're weeping that the criminal who murdered him is still alive.

Therefore have done. Some grief shows much of love;

But much of grief shows still some want of wit.[16]

Juliet.

75   Yet let me weep for such a feeling loss.[17]

Lady Capulet.

    So shall you feel the loss, but not the friend

    Which you weep for.

Juliet.   Feeling so the loss,

    I cannot choose but ever weep the friend.

Lady Capulet.

    Well, girl, thou weep'st not so much for his death

80   As that the villain lives which slaughtered him.

> **IN OTHER WORDS**   Lady Capulet arrives, seeing Juliet's distress. She thinks that Juliet is still crying for her dead cousin, Tybalt. She tells Juliet that grieving will not bring Tybalt back, and she should stop. Then she suggests that the real cause of Juliet's grief is that Romeo, her cousin's killer, is still alive.

Juliet.

    What villain, madam?

Lady Capulet.   That same villain Romeo.

Juliet *(aside).*

    Villain and he be many miles asunder[18]—

    God pardon him! I do, with all my heart;

    And yet no man like he doth grieve my heart.

Lady Capulet.

85   That is because the traitor murderer lives.

Juliet.

    Ay, madam, from the reach of these my hands.

    Would none but I might venge my cousin's death!

---

16. **wit:** mental balance.
17. **feeling loss:** loss so deeply felt.
18. **asunder:** apart.

Lady Capulet.

> We will have vengeance for it, fear thou not.
>
> Then weep no more. I'll send to one in Mantua,
>
> 90 Where that same banished runagate[19] doth live,
>
> Shall give him such an unaccustomed dram[20]
>
> That he shall soon keep Tybalt company;
>
> And then I hope thou wilt be satisfied.

Juliet.

> Indeed I never shall be satisfied
>
> 95 With Romeo till I behold him—dead—
>
> Is my poor heart so for a kinsman vexed.
>
> Madam, if you could find out but a man
>
> To bear a poison, I would temper[21] it—
>
> That Romeo should, upon receipt thereof,
>
> 100 Soon sleep in quiet. O, how my heart abhors
>
> To hear him named and cannot come to him,
>
> To wreak[22] the love I bore my cousin
>
> Upon his body that hath slaughtered him!

Lady Capulet.

> Find thou the means, and I'll find such a man.
>
> 105 But now I'll tell thee joyful tidings,[23] girl.

Juliet.

> And joy comes well in such a needy time.
>
> What are they, I beseech your ladyship?

IN OTHER WORDS Juliet admits that Romeo is indeed the cause of her grief. Lady Capulet, thinking Juliet hates Romeo, suggests finding someone to poison him. A conversation full of double meanings follows, as Juliet answers in a way that expresses her true feelings for Romeo while keeping the truth from her mother. Then Lady Capulet tells Juliet she has some good news.

---

19. **runagate:** fugitive.
20. **unaccustomed dram:** unexpected drink (of poison).
21. **temper:** mix (she really means "weaken").
22. **wreak:** avenge (she really means "express").
23. **tidings:** news.

Your TURN

DRAMATIC IRONY

Lines 94–96 contain a double meaning. Lady Capulet hears that Juliet wants to see Romeo "dead." But what does the audience know Juliet really means?

_____

_____

_____

_____

_____

Here's HOW

VOCABULARY

The word *abhors* in line 100 is new to me. But, I think I can figure out the meaning. Juliet says her heart feels this way when it hears Romeo's name and cannot come to him. I think *abhors* means "hates"—that makes sense.

Lady Capulet.

Well, well, thou hast a careful[24] father, child;

One who, to put thee from thy heaviness,

110   Hath sorted out[25] a sudden day of joy

That thou expects not nor I looked not for.

Juliet.

Madam, in happy time![26] What day is that?

Lady Capulet.

Marry, my child, early next Thursday morn

The gallant, young, and noble gentleman,

115   The County Paris, at Saint Peter's Church,

Shall happily make thee there a joyful bride.

Juliet.

Now by Saint Peter's Church, and Peter too,

He shall not make me there a joyful bride!

I wonder at this haste, that I must wed

120   Ere he that should be husband comes to woo.

I pray you tell my lord and father, madam,

I will not marry yet; and when I do, I swear

It shall be Romeo, whom you know I hate,

Rather than Paris. These are news indeed!

Lady Capulet.

125   Here comes your father. Tell him so yourself,

And see how he will take it at your hands.

[*Enter* CAPULET *and* NURSE.]

Capulet.

When the sun sets the earth doth drizzle dew,

But for the sunset of my brother's son

It rains downright.

130   How now? A conduit,[27] girl? What, still in tears?

Evermore showering? In one little body

---

24. **careful:** full of caring (for Juliet).
25. **sorted out:** selected.
26. **in happy time:** at a lucky time.
27. **conduit:** water pipe (Juliet is weeping).

Thou counterfeits a bark,[28] a sea, a wind:

For still thy eyes, which I may call the sea,

Do ebb and flow with tears; the bark thy body is,

135   Sailing in this salt flood; the winds, thy sighs,

Who, raging with thy tears and they with them,

Without a sudden calm will overset

Thy tempest-tossèd body. How now, wife?

Have you delivered to her our decree?[29]

Lady Capulet.

140   Ay, sir; but she will none, she gives you thanks.

I would the fool were married to her grave!

> **IN OTHER WORDS**   Lady Capulet announces that Juliet's father, to cheer her up, has set a date for her to marry Paris: next Thursday. Juliet says to tell him that she doesn't want to marry Paris. Lady Capulet, annoyed, says she can tell him herself. Lord Capulet and the nurse come in. Seeing Juliet in tears, he also assumes she is still crying for Tybalt. He asks his wife if she has told Juliet about the wedding, and she angrily replies that Juliet has refused.

Capulet.

Soft! Take me with you,[30] take me with you, wife.

How? Will she none? Doth she not give us thanks?

Is she not proud? Doth she not count her blest,

145   Unworthy as she is, that we have wrought[31]

So worthy a gentleman to be her bride?

Juliet.

Not proud you have, but thankful that you have.

Proud can I never be of what I hate,

But thankful even for hate that is meant love.

Capulet.

150   How, how, how, how, chopped-logic?[32] What is this?

---

28. **counterfeits a bark:** imitates a boat.
29. **decree:** decision.
30. **Soft! Take me with you:** Wait! Let me understand you.
31. **wrought:** arranged.
32. **chopped-logic:** hair-splitting.

Your TURN

PARAPHRASING

Paraphrase in your own words Lady Capulet's response to her husband in lines 140–141.

_____

_____

_____

_____

_____

_____

_____

_____

_____

_____

_____

Here's HOW

PARAPHRASING

This is how I'd paraphrase Juliet's response to her father in lines 147–149: I'm not proud that you've arranged for me to be married, but I'm thankful that you care about me enough to have done so. I can't be proud of something I hate, but I know that you meant it in love.

VOCABULARY

In line 156, Lord Capulet threatens to drag Juliet to the church on a hurdle. The word *hurdle* can mean either a "barrier that a runner must jump over in a race" or "a sled that transports criminals to be executed." Underline the meaning that is correct here.

PARAPHRASING

How would you paraphrase lines 159–160?

_____

_____

_____

_____

_____

DRAMATIC IRONY

Lord Capulet says that if Juliet doesn't obey him, he never wants to see her again (lines 162–163). How does this show dramatic irony—since you know how the play turns out?

_____

_____

_____

_____

_____

_____

"Proud"—and "I thank you"—and "I thank you not"—

And yet "not proud"? Mistress minion[33] you,

Thank me no thankings, nor proud me no prouds,

But fettle[34] your fine joints 'gainst Thursday next

155   To go with Paris to Saint Peter's Church,

Or I will drag thee on a hurdle thither.

Out, you greensickness carrion![35] Out, you baggage!

You tallow-face!

Lady Capulet.   Fie, fie! What, are you mad?

Juliet.

Good father, I beseech you on my knees,

160   Hear me with patience but to speak a word.

Capulet.

Hang thee, young baggage! Disobedient wretch!

I tell thee what—get thee to church a' Thursday

Or never after look me in the face.

Speak not, reply not, do not answer me!

165   My fingers itch. Wife, we scarce thought us blest

That God had lent us but this only child;

But now I see this one is one too much,

And that we have a curse in having her.

Out on her, hilding![36]

Nurse.   God in heaven bless her!

170   You are to blame, my lord, to rate[37] her so.

IN OTHER WORDS Lord Capulet is shocked by Juliet's refusal. He expected her to be pleased and grateful at being given such a good husband. Juliet thanks him for his good intentions, but says she hates the idea of marrying Paris. Her father flies into a rage and says she will be at the church on Thursday, or he will drag her there. Ignoring Juliet's pleading, he says if she will not marry Paris he never wants to see her again. The nurse tells him he is wrong to scold Juliet so harshly.

---

33. minion: badly behaved girl.
34. fettle: make ready.
35. carrion: a decaying dead animal.
36. hilding: horrible person.
37. rate: scold.

Capulet.

>And why, my Lady Wisdom? Hold your tongue,
>
>Good Prudence. Smatter with your gossips,[38] go!

Nurse.

>I speak no treason.

Capulet.   O, God-i-god-en![39]

Nurse.

>May not one speak?

Capulet.   Peace, you mumbling fool!

175
>Utter your gravity o'er a gossip's bowl,
>
>For here we need it not.

Lady Capulet.   You are too hot.

Capulet.

>God's bread![40] It makes me mad.
>
>Day, night; hour, tide, time; work, play;
>
>Alone, in company; still my care hath been

180
>To have her matched; and having now provided
>
>A gentleman of noble parentage,
>
>Of fair demesnes,[41] youthful, and nobly trained,
>
>Stuffed, as they say, with honorable parts,
>
>Proportioned as one's thought would wish a man—

185
>And then to have a wretched puling[42] fool,
>
>A whining mammet,[43] in her fortune's tender,[44]
>
>To answer "I'll not wed, I cannot love;
>
>I am too young, I pray you pardon me"!
>
>But, and you will not wed, I'll pardon you![45]

190
>Graze where you will, you shall not house with me.
>
>Look to't, think on't; I do not use to jest.
>
>Thursday is near; lay hand on heart, advise.[46]
>
>And you be mine, I'll give you to my friend;
>
>And you be not, hang, beg, starve, die in the streets,

Here's HOW

VOCABULARY

I have heard of the word *treason* in line 173, but I'm not sure what it means. As I read other words around it, I think it means something like "lies." But my dictionary says *treason* means "betrayal."

Your TURN

VOCABULARY

The word *gravity* can mean either "force that draws all bodies toward the earth's center," "seriousness," or, sometimes in Shakespeare's day, "matter of importance." Which meaning is correct in line 175?

_____

_____

_____

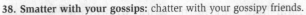

38. **Smatter with your gossips:** chatter with your gossipy friends.
39. **God-i-god-en!:** Get on with you! ("God give you good evening.")
40. **God's bread!:** oath on the sacrament of Communion.
41. **of fair demesnes** (dih MAYN): holding much property and land.
42. **puling** (PYOOL eeng): whining.
43. **mammet:** puppet.
44. **in her fortune's tender:** with all her good fortunes.
45. **I'll pardon you!:** I'll give you permission to go!
46. **advise:** consider.

TURN

VOCABULARY

The word *monument* can mean either a "tomb" or a "marker to honor a dead person." Which meaning is correct in line 203?

_____

_____

_____

Your

TURN

PARAPHRASING

How would you paraphrase lines 204–205?

_____

_____

_____

_____

_____

_____

_____

_____

195   For, by my soul, I'll ne'er acknowledge thee,

Nor what is mine shall never do thee good.

Trust to't. Bethink you. I'll not be forsworn.⁴⁷ [*Exit.*]

IN OTHER WORDS   Lord Capulet does not want to listen to the nurse, either. He is furious. He put great effort into finding Juliet a good husband, and his ungrateful, whining daughter will not have Paris. If she refuses to marry Paris, Lord Capulet will disown her and throw her out on the street. He storms out.

Juliet.

Is there no pity sitting in the clouds

That sees into the bottom of my grief?

200   O sweet my mother, cast me not away!

Delay this marriage for a month, a week;

Or if you do not, make the bridal bed

In that dim monument where Tybalt lies.

Lady Capulet.

Talk not to me, for I'll not speak a word.

205   Do as thou wilt, for I have done with thee.   [*Exit.*]

Juliet.

O God!—O nurse, how shall this be prevented?

My husband is on earth, my faith in heaven.⁴⁸

How shall that faith return again to earth

Unless that husband send it me from heaven

210   By leaving earth? Comfort me, counsel me.

Alack, alack, that heaven should practice stratagems⁴⁹

Upon so soft a subject as myself!

What say'st thou? Hast thou not a word of joy?

Some comfort, nurse.

Nurse.   Faith, here it is.

215   Romeo is banished; and all the world to nothing⁵⁰

That he dares ne'er come back to challenge you;

---

47. **forsworn:** guilty of breaking my vow.
48. **my faith in heaven:** my wedding vow is recorded in heaven.
49. **stratagems:** tricks.
50. **all the world to nothing:** it is a safe bet.

Or if he do, it needs must be by stealth.

Then, since the case so stands as now it doth,

I think it best you married with the county.

220   O, he's a lovely gentleman!

Romeo's a dishclout[51] to him. An eagle, madam,

Hath not so green, so quick, so fair an eye

As Paris hath. Beshrew[52] my very heart,

I think you are happy in this second match,

225   For it excels your first; or if it did not,

Your first is dead—or 'twere as good he were

As living here and you no use of him.

Juliet.

    Speak'st thou from thy heart?

Nurse.

    And from my soul too; else beshrew them both.

> **IN OTHER WORDS**   Juliet begs her mother to delay the wedding. Lady Capulet says she wants nothing to do with her, and leaves. Alone with the nurse, Juliet is frantic. How can she marry Paris, when her husband is still living? The nurse tells her that Romeo is banished, which is as good as dead; she should marry the handsome Paris, who will make her happy.

Juliet.

230   Amen!

Nurse.

    What?

Juliet.

    Well, thou hast comforted me marvelous much.

Go in; and tell my lady I am gone,

Having displeased my father, to Laurence' cell,

235   To make confession and to be absolved.[53]

---

51. **dishclout:** literally dishcloth; limp and weak.
52. **Beshrew:** curse.
53. **To make confession and to be absolved:** to tell sins to a priest and ask for forgiveness.

   THE TRAGEDY OF ROMEO AND JULIET, ACT III, SCENE 5   **175**

Here's HOW

VOCABULARY

The word *stealth* in line 217 sounds familiar. I have heard of "stealth fighters"—warplanes with technology that keeps them hidden from the enemy. I think *stealth* must mean "secret."

Your TURN

DRAMATIC IRONY

Why is it ironic that the nurse says in line 226 that Romeo is as good as dead?

_____

_____

_____

_____

_____

_____

_____

_____

_____

Your TURN

VOCABULARY

The word *fiend* in line 237 looks like the word *friend.* But the meanings of these words couldn't be more different from each other. Circle the word that shows you that *fiend* is the opposite of *friend.* In fact, a *fiend* is a demon or cruel person.

Nurse.

> Marry, I will; and this is wisely done.   [*Exit.*]

Juliet.

> Ancient damnation![54] O most wicked fiend!
>
> Is it more sin to wish me thus forsworn,
>
> Or to dispraise[55] my lord with that same tongue
>
> 240 Which she hath praised him with above compare
>
> So many thousand times? Go, counselor!
>
> Thou and my bosom henceforth shall be twain.[56]
>
> I'll to the friar to know his remedy.[57]
>
> If all else fail, myself have power to die.   [*Exit.*]

IN OTHER WORDS Juliet is disgusted with the nurse's advice. She tells her she is going to Friar Laurence to confess her sin of having angered her father. The nurse leaves, and Juliet says that she will never again trust this woman. The nurse first praised Romeo and now wants Juliet to betray him. Juliet will go to Friar Laurence and ask his advice. If there is no other answer, she will kill herself.

---

54. **Ancient damnation!:** Damned old woman!
55. **dispraise:** take away the praises from.
56. **twain:** separate.
57. **remedy:** solution.

Paraphrasing

Paraphrasing means restating text in your own words. When you paraphrase, it makes the text easier to understand. Remember these tips when you paraphrase:

- Make sure you understand the main idea of the text.
- Look up unfamiliar words.
- Replace difficult words with simple ones.
- Restate figures of speech in your own words, making the comparison clear.

Fill in the chart below to practice paraphrasing. In the left column are passages from the play. Paraphrase the passages in the right column. Before you begin, remember to check each passage for footnotes. One paraphrase has been done for you.

Passage from Play	Paraphrase
1. "Evermore weeping for your cousin's death? / What, wilt thou wash him from his grave with tears?" (lines 70–71)	
2. "O, how my heart abhors / To hear him named and cannot come to him." (lines 100–101)	
3. "Delay this marriage for a month, a week; / Or if you do not, make the bridal bed / In that dim monument where Tybalt lies." (lines 201–203)	Put off this marriage for a month or even a week. If you won't, you may as well put my marriage bed in the tomb with Tybalt.
4. "Alack, alack, that heaven should practice stratagems / Upon so soft a subject as myself!" (lines 211–212)	

From The Tragedy of Romeo and Juliet
Act IV, Scene 3

Literary Focus: Soliloquy

A **soliloquy** (suh LIHL uh kwee) is a long speech by a character alone
on the stage. In this speech the character tells about his or her
thoughts and feelings out loud. The soliloquy gives the audience a
chance to hear what the character is thinking. Modern plays seldom
use soliloquies, but you can find some of Shakespeare's most beautiful
poetry, as well as some of his most famous lines, in his soliloquies.

To be or not
to be...

Reading Skill: Making Inferences

Reading well takes lots of brain power. This is because writers don't
state directly everything you need to understand the text. You have
to figure out the meaning by **making inferences,** or educated guesses,
based on information in the text and on your own experiences.

Into the Play

Shakespeare wrote his plays more than 400 years ago, yet they are
still popular today. In fact, almost thirty movies released between
2000 and 2002 list William Shakespeare as the writer. What is the
secret of Shakespeare's timeless appeal? First, the plays deal with
powerful human emotions such as love, revenge, loyalty, and
betrayal. Second, the plays' action can be set almost anywhere.
Modern New York City, 1930s Italy, ancient Japan—all these have
been used as settings for Shakespeare's works. Pretend you are a
director. Where and when would you set Romeo and Juliet?

The Tragedy of Romeo and Juliet

Act IV, Scene 3

William Shakespeare

Act IV, Scene 3

YOU NEED TO KNOW Juliet pretends to obey her father and says that she will now marry Paris. Actually, she plans to drink a potion given to her by Friar Laurence the night before the wedding. The potion will make her appear dead. Then she will be taken to the family tomb, where Romeo will meet her when she awakes. Her nurse, unaware of this plan, is helping Juliet prepare for her wedding to Paris in the morning.

Scene 3. *Juliet's chamber.*

Enter JULIET *and* NURSE.

Juliet.

Ay, those attires are best; but, gentle nurse,

I pray thee leave me to myself tonight;

For I have need of many orisons[1]

To move the heavens to smile upon my state,

5   Which, well thou knowest, is cross and full of sin.

[*Enter* LADY CAPULET.]

Lady Capulet.

What, are you busy, ho? Need you my help?

Juliet.

No, madam; we have culled[2] such necessaries

As are behoveful[3] for our state[4] tomorrow.

So please you, let me now be left alone,

10   And let the nurse this night sit up with you;

For I am sure you have your hands full all

In this so sudden business.

Lady Capulet.   Good night.

Get thee to bed, and rest; for thou hast need.

[*Exeunt* LADY CAPULET *and* NURSE.]

---

1. **orisons:** prayers.
2. **culled:** picked out.
3. **behoveful:** suitable.
4. **state:** ceremonies.

Juliet.

Farewell! God knows when we shall meet again.

15 I have a faint cold fear thrills through my veins

That almost freezes up the heat of life.

I'll call them back again to comfort me.

Nurse!—What should she do here?

My dismal scene I needs must act alone.

20 Come, vial.[5]

What if this mixture do not work at all?

Shall I be married then tomorrow morning?

No, no! This shall forbid it. Lie thou there.

[*Lays down a dagger.*]

IN OTHER WORDS   Tomorrow is the wedding. Juliet asks her mother and nurse to leave her alone for the evening, so she can pray. Alone, Juliet faces her fears. What if the potion doesn't work? Will she have to marry Paris in the morning? No—she has a dagger ready and would stab herself first.

What if it be a poison which the friar

25 Subtly hath ministered[6] to have me dead,

Lest[7] in this marriage he should be dishonored

Because he married me before to Romeo?

I fear it is; and yet methinks it should not,

For he hath still been tried[8] a holy man.

30 How if, when I am laid into the tomb,

I wake before the time that Romeo

Come to redeem me? There's a fearful point!

Shall I not then be stifled[9] in the vault,

To whose foul mouth no healthsome air breathes in,

35 And there die strangled ere my Romeo comes?

Or, if I live, is it not very like

The horrible conceit[10] of death and night,

---

5. **vial:** small bottle that holds liquid.
6. **ministered:** provided.
7. **Lest:** for fear that.
8. **still been tried:** always been proved.
9. **stifled:** suffocated.
10. **conceit:** idea.

Your TURN

MAKING INFERENCES

What is Juliet talking about in line 23? You'll find the answer in the stage direction below the line. Write what she means in your own words on the lines below.

_____

_____

_____

_____

Your TURN

SOLILOQUY

In this soliloquy Juliet expresses two main fears about the potion she is going to take. The first one is that it won't work. Circle the words in lines 24–29 that describe the second fear.

Here's HOW

SOLILOQUY

Lines 30–35 show Juliet's fear of what she's about to do. There are so many things that could go wrong! I can identify with her—I would be terrified to wake up by myself in a tomb.

In lines 36–57 Juliet jumps from thought to thought without resolving any of them. What does this suggest about her state of mind?

_____

_____

_____

VOCABULARY

The word _spit_ can mean either "eject saliva from one's mouth" or "spear." Which meaning is correct in line 56?

_____

_____

MAKING INFERENCES

This scene is so sad. I know Juliet doesn't die now and that she dies at the end of the play in a tomb. So maybe her fears about the poison are misplaced, but she certainly has good reasons to be afraid!

Together with the terror of the place—

As in a vault, an ancient receptacle[11]

40   Where for this many hundred years the bones

Of all my buried ancestors are packed;

Where bloody Tybalt, yet but green in earth,[12]

Lies fest'ring[13] in his shroud; where, as they say,

At some hours in the night spirits resort—

45   Alack, alack, is it not like that I,

So early waking—what with loathsome smells,

And shrieks like mandrakes[14] torn out of the earth,

That living mortals, hearing them, run mad—

I, if I wake, shall I not be distraught,

50   Environèd[15] with all these hideous fears,

And madly play with my forefathers' joints,

And pluck the mangled Tybalt from his shroud,

And, in this rage, with some great kinsman's bone

As with a club dash out my desp'rate brains?

55   O, look! Methinks I see my cousin's ghost

Seeking out Romeo, that did spit his body

Upon a rapier's[16] point. Stay, Tybalt, stay!

Romeo, Romeo, Romeo, I drink to thee.

[_She falls upon her bed within the curtains._]

IN OTHER WORDS   Juliet's fears continue. What if Friar Laurence has given her poison so that no one will discover he married her to Romeo in secret? What if she suffocates in the tomb before Romeo arrives? Or, what if she awakens next to Tybalt's corpse and her ancestors' bones and the terror drives her insane? What if her cousin's ghost wants revenge on Romeo? At last, she drinks the potion and falls unconscious.

---

11. **receptacle:** container.
12. **green in earth:** newly buried.
13. **fest'ring:** decaying.
14. **mandrakes:** plants resembling the human body that were said to scream when pulled up.
15. **Environèd:** surrounded.
16. **rapier's:** sword's.

Soliloquy

A **soliloquy** is a long speech by a character alone on the stage. In this speech the character expresses his or her thoughts out loud. This allows the audience a chance to hear what that character is thinking and feeling.

Each of Juliet's questions in the soliloquy builds in emotion, showing that her terror is growing. Read the passages listed on the left in the chart below. Remember to consult the footnotes for unfamiliar words. In the middle column, write a brief summary of each passage in your own words. In the right-hand column, comment briefly on Juliet's state of mind. The first one has been done for you.

Passage	Summary	Juliet's State of Mind
1. "What if it be a poison which the friar / Subtly hath ministered to have me dead, / Lest in this marriage he should be dishonored / Because he married me before to Romeo?" (lines 24–27)	What if Friar Laurence has given me poison in order to save his own reputation?	Juliet is becoming worried.
2. "How if, when I am laid into the tomb, / I wake before the time that Romeo / Come to redeem me? There's a fearful point!" (lines 30–32)		
3. "O, look! Methinks I see my cousin's ghost / Seeking out Romeo, that did spit his body / Upon a rapier's point. Stay, Tybalt, stay!" (lines 55–57)		

Romeo and Juliet in Bosnia

Reading Skill: Making Connections

Have you ever read a story that seemed familiar? Maybe it reminded you of another story. Or maybe it even reminded you of a personal experience. When you ask yourself how a story is like or unlike another story or experience, you are **making connections.** Often, we connect with stories about love, loss, friendship, or betrayal. These concerns are common to all people, no matter where or when we live. Making connections helps you better understand the subject.

Making Connections

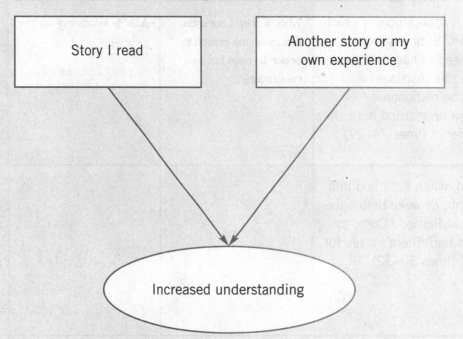

Story I read

Another story or my own experience

Increased understanding

Into the Editorial

An editorial is a story that presents opinions of the writer. Editorials are common in newspapers and newsmagazines. They are often used to present an editor's opinion of a current news event. In "Romeo and Juliet in Bosnia," the editorial writer uses a tragic story to present his opinion about war.

Romeo and Juliet in Bosnia

Bob Herbert

BASED ON THE EDITORIAL

FROM *The New York Times,* May 8, 1994

Your
TURN

MAKING CONNECTIONS

Re-read lines 12–14. Find
another similarity between this
story and *Romeo and Juliet.*
Describe it on the lines below.

_____

_____

_____

_____

Your
TURN

MAKING CONNECTIONS

Take a look at lines 29–32.
What connection does the
writer make between this story
and all wars?

_____

_____

_____

_____

One Tuesday night *Frontline*[1] presented the true story of Bosko
Brkic, an Eastern Orthodox Serb, and Admira Ismic, a Muslim.[2] They
met in the mid-1980s, fell in love, and died together in Sarajevo.[3]

5   The documentary "Romeo and Juliet in Saravejo" focuses on
thoroughly human people caught up in a horror. It's one thing to hear
about the bloodshed caused by war, but it's different to actually
witness a parent search for meaning while recalling a lost daughter.

The shock of their story is that they could be a young couple from
anywhere. They graduated from high school in June of 1986, and they
10   both were crazy about movies and music. Admira had a cat named
Yellow that she loved and Bosko liked to play practical jokes.

Admira's father says he had nothing against the relationship. He
says he had started to love Bosko. But Admira's grandmother opposed
it: "He is Serb, she is a Muslim, and how will it work?"

15   For Admira and Bosko, love was the answer. While Bosko was
away on his required military service, Admira wrote that they would
soon be reunited. "After that, absolutely nothing can separate us."

The 1984 Winter Olympics had just been held in Sarajevo. People
were trying to live together in peace in this cosmopolitan city of
20   Serbs, Croats, Muslims, Jews, and others. But people who hated those
of different backgrounds and religions shattered the peace of Sarajevo.
Bosko was faced with a cruel choice. He could not kill Serbs, his own
people, and he could not fire on his girlfriend's people.

Bosko and Admira decided to escape from Sarajevo. They had to
25   cross a bridge between the Serb and Muslim lines. Gunmen from both
sides overlooked the bridge. No one knows who shot the lovers, but
onlookers said that Bosko died instantly. Admira crawled to him and
died a few minutes later.

Only the times and places change. Various reasons are given for
30   the endless conflicts. If you dig a little, you will uncover ethnic or
religious reasons. The world stands helpless before the madness,
which is not the curse of our times but of all time.

---

1. *Frontline:* a PBS television series that presents in-depth news features.
2. **Serb … Muslim:** people of different race and religion who were at war during this time.
3. **Sarajevo** (SAHR uh YAY voh): capital of Bosnia and Herzegovina.

From "In America; Romeo and Juliet in Bosnia" by Bob Herbert adapted *from The New York
Times,* May 8, 1994. Copyright © 1994 by The New York Times Agency. Retold by Holt,
Rinehart and Winston. Reproduced by permission of **The New York Times Agency.**

Making Connections

Most of us make connections between sources without even thinking about it. A song has special meaning for us because it reminds us of someone. Or a story reminds us of something that happened in our family. By **making connections,** we gain a better understanding of a subject.

In the chart below, make three connections between "Romeo and Juliet in Bosnia" and some other work. The first column lists events from this informational piece. In the second column, list a similar event from a story you've read or seen, or a song you've heard. You can use a different connecting work for each event. One connection has been made for you.

Event in "Romeo and Juliet in Bosnia"	Event in Connecting Work
1. A Serb and Muslim fall in love. These racial and religious groups are at war.	Connecting work: the movie *Titanic* Event: Two unlikely people fall in love. The girl is rich, and the boy is poor.
2. Two lovers die together.	Connecting work: Event:
3. Life is disrupted by civil war.	Connecting work: Event:

AUTHOR AND TITLE INDEX